PRAISE FOR LONGE ....

"As someone who has spent the past decade redefining what 'ageing' looks like – on the road, on the trails, and across the world's toughest endurance races – I am always searching for wisdom that aligns with what I have lived through my own body.

Dr Mak's *Longe-Vitality* does exactly that.

Jens presents ageing not as a decline, but as a river in motion – energetic at its source, adapting to obstacles, and flowing with purpose all the way to its destination. As I continue to compete and break Australian and world records into my late 60s and 70s, this metaphor rings profoundly true. A river remains vibrant when it keeps moving, so do we.

What sets this book apart is Jens's ability to weave rigorous science with inspiring human stories. He explains, with clarity and compassion, how consistent, mindful movement supports not only the longevity of our muscles, bones, and cardiovascular system, but also the vitality of our brain. Every chapter is enriched with anecdotes – real people who embody the research and prove what is possible.

His Run Doc's *Longe-Vitality* tips are practical, powerful, and grounded in evidence. They mirror the principles that have allowed me to set Australian single-age records from 67 to 70, to hold multiple national age-group records from half marathon to 50 km, and to break the Grand Master

70+ women's record at the Comrades Marathon by over an hour – finishing ahead of every man in my category and all but one woman who was a decade younger.

This book is fascinating, hopeful, and deeply motivating. Whether you are an athlete, a weekend walker, or someone simply wanting to age with strength and agency, *Longe-Vitality* will show you that the river can keep running, for as long as you choose to move with it."

Jennifer Kellett
Australian single-age record holder (67, 68, 69, 70)
Australian 65 to 69 age-group record holder –
half marathon, marathon, 50 km
World single-age marathon record (69 years)
2024 Comrades Marathon Women's 70+ record holder

"At 77, running isn't just something I do – it's the way I live. It keeps me young, mobile, connected, and constantly inspired. Through running, I've met extraordinary people around the world who share the same passion, and it has given me a life defined by dedication, discipline, and determination. That's why Dr Mak's *Longe-Vitality* resonates so strongly with me.

This book captures what I've experienced firsthand across decades of competitive running and multiple world records: ageing isn't a sentence – it's an opportunity. Jens brings together the science of healthy ageing with real-world stories that show how movement, purpose, nutrition, sleep, and mindset can keep us thriving well into our later years.

I train 6 days a week, averaging 50 miles, and continue to race internationally, most recently earning six gold medals at the 2024 World Masters Athletics Championships in Gothenburg. As I look ahead to competing in Daegu in 2026, I know that consistency, a healthy diet, proper hydration, and good sleep are the foundations that keep me strong. *Longe-Vitality* explains these principles beautifully and empowers readers to apply them in their own lives.

Jens has written a book that's both scientifically grounded and deeply motivating. Whether you're an athlete or simply someone who wants to age with strength, joy, and purpose, *Longe-Vitality* will show you what's possible when you choose to keep moving."

Jeannie Rice
World record holder (5 km to marathon)
6 times gold medallist – World Masters Athletics
Championships, Gothenburg 2024
Retired real estate agent

LONGE-VITALITY

LONGE-VITALITY

VITALITY

The New Science and Soul of
Forging a Long Vital Life

DR JENSON MAK

First published in 2025 by Dean Publishing
PO Box 119
Mt. Macedon, Victoria, 3441
Australia
deanpublishing.com

DEAN PUBLISHING

Cataloguing-in-Publication Data
National Library of Australia
Title: Longe-Vitality: The New Science and Soul of Forging a Long Vital Life
Edition: 1st edn
ISBN: 978-0-648995-79-1
Category: Health & fitness/Longevity

The information contained in this book is provided for general educational and informational purposes only. It is not intended to constitute medical advice, healthcare advice, diagnosis, or treatment for any individual. Nothing in this publication should be interpreted as creating a practitioner–patient relationship or as a substitute for consultation with a qualified healthcare professional.

Readers should seek the advice of a registered medical practitioner or other appropriately qualified healthcare provider in relation to any questions or concerns regarding their health, medical conditions, or before commencing any exercise, dietary, or lifestyle changes.

Although every effort has been made to ensure the accuracy and currency of the information at the time of publication, healthcare knowledge and scientific guidance evolve regularly. The author and publisher make no representations or warranties, express or implied, regarding the completeness, reliability, or suitability of the content for any particular purpose.

The author and publisher disclaim all liability for any loss, damage, injury, or adverse consequences—whether direct, indirect, incidental, consequential, or otherwise—arising from the use of, reliance on, or application of any information contained in this book.

Any examples, case studies, or anecdotes included are provided solely for illustrative purposes and do not guarantee or predict similar outcomes. Readers assume full responsibility for their decisions and actions.

As I put the finishing touches on my third book, *Longe-Vitality* (that's longe- as in longevity), I can't help but reflect on one of the most exhilarating and humbling experiences of my life so far. Just days ago, I crossed the finish line of the inaugural Ultra-Trail Australia Miler (UTAM), a 162-kilometre ultra-endurance adventure through the brutal yet breathtaking terrain of the UNESCO-listed Blue Mountains.

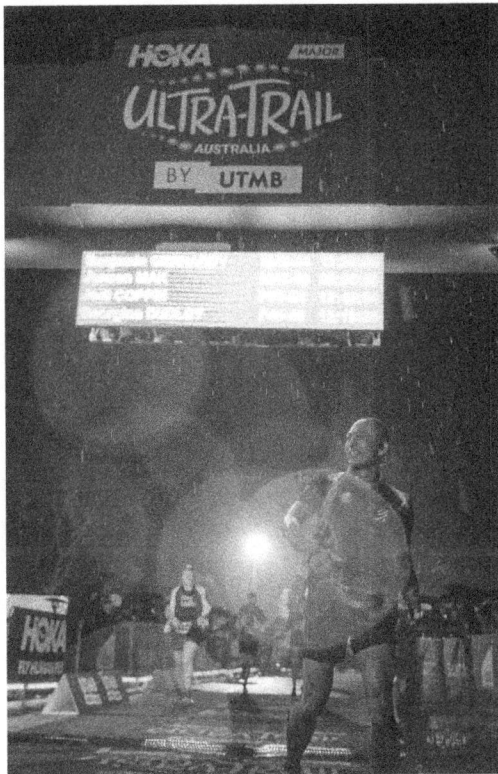

2025 Finisher, Inaugural Ultra-trail Australia Miler
(100-miles) Finisher, 241st Place.

Over 2 days – 16 and 17 May 2025 – I ran an epic journey from the Grand Canyon car park, climbing the infamous 951 Furber Steps and finishing at Scenic World in pouring rain. The UTAM isn't just any ultra; it's one of the toughest and most iconic trail events on the planet and a major race in the UTMB Asia-Pacific circuit. Out of 400 brave entrants (374 starters), I placed 241st, finishing with equal parts exhaustion and euphoria alongside my incredible Sydney Striders and Coogee Run Club mates. It was more than just a race; it was a spiritual test of grit, grace, and gratitude.

This book is dedicated to the warrior spirit of my late mother, Demi, whose mantra *"kia kaha"* (stay strong) echoed through my every step, especially when I stood at the start line nursing a lumbar disc injury and when I rolled my ankle just 8 km into the race. Mum taught me not just to push through, but to connect deeply: with people, with purpose, and with myself. Her wisdom in communication and compassion continues to guide me, even now.

I also dedicate this book to my grandma, F Leung, who went to heaven in August 2025. Throughout her life and especially at the amazing age of 101, she showed enormous grit and undoubtedly shaped me into the person I am today.

I also dedicate *Longe-Vitality* to my dad, Andy – my loudest cheerleader and proudest supporter. And to my partner in crime, Louise, the real-life Louise Sawyer to my Thelma. She knows just what to say and when to say it to fire up this old engine. To our children, Johann, Jacinta, and Leonardo – thank you for being my reason to keep moving forward. It has been the greatest joy pacing each of you in your races, especially Jacinta in her second HOKA Sydney Half Marathon and Johann in his debut this year. You've shown me that legacy starts at home.

And finally, I wish to honour and pay my respects to the traditional custodians of the lands on which I've trained, particularly the *Guringai* people of *Garigal* Country. I acknowledge the Elders past and present, and extend that respect to all Aboriginal and Torres Strait Islander peoples. Your connection to land, movement, and story has inspired me deeply.

Now lace up, *Longe-Vitality* begins here,
with heart, soul, and a few blisters.

TABLE OF CONTENTS

INTRODUCTION

OUR JOURNEY BEGINS...

"Life has no remote ... get up and change it yourself!"

– Mark A Cooper

The air was cool, and there was the kind of pre-dawn stillness that carries both nerves and promise. I stood at the start line of a race that would test everything I thought I knew about myself. It was my first 100-miler. To my left was a man in his 20s, earbuds in, bouncing on his toes like a caged spring. To my right stood a woman in her 70s, weathered, calm, and smiling. She adjusted her cap and simply said, "Beautiful day for a long run, isn't it?"

In that moment, I felt the full weight of my own transformation. Not long before, I was the 'Fat Doc', a medical professional giving advice I wasn't truly living. My body was heavy, my spirit sluggish, my own healthspan (the period of living in good health) quietly eroding. Back then, running 100 miles would have seemed like madness. Yet here I was, shoulder to shoulder with someone who had defied the script society writes for ageing. She wasn't there to 'manage decline'. She was there to run, joyfully, powerfully, without apology.

The gun went off, and as we shuffled forward together, I realised this race wasn't just about distance. It was about destiny. Hers, mine, and perhaps yours.

Nowadays, we're living longer than ever. But too often, ageing is framed as a slow march towards loss – loss of mobility, independence, meaning. The narrative is one of limitation, of inevitability. Yet as I discovered both through medicine and my own rebirth as an endurance runner, that narrative is dangerously incomplete. What if ageing wasn't a slow fade, but a chance to burn brighter? What if it was an invitation to move, to grow, to connect, to thrive?

That's the heart of *Longe-Vitality.*

This book is about those who dare to believe life doesn't stop at 40, 60, or 80. It's about the Sister Madonna Buders of the world, the 'Iron Nun' who laced up her first pair of running shoes at 52 and went on to complete dozens of Ironman Triathlons. It's about my grandmothers, who built health not through laboratories or gyms, but through daily acts of movement, care, and service. And it's about everyday runners and walkers: the neighbour training for their first 5 km, the retiree rediscovering hiking, the middle-aged parent who finally decides to put their own wellbeing first. But more than that, it's about you. If you've ever suspected that your best days might still lie ahead, even if your knees creak or your hair has silvered, you're in the right place.

When I trained for and completed my first 100-miler, it wasn't just my body that changed. It was my story. Each step stripped away an old identity – the fatigued, unhealthy version of me – and replaced it with something stronger, steadier, and more resilient. Out there in the dark hours of the night, and in the later portion of the race, when my legs screamed, my stomach turned, and I was turning into a running zombie, I realised something vital: longevity isn't about avoiding suffering. It's about choosing struggle that strengthens. Running taught me that ageing can be the same.

When we lean into purposeful movement, we don't just add years to our lives; we add life to our years.

That's why I no longer see ageing as decline. I see it as a long-distance run worth training for. Medicine has much to offer in preventing and treating disease, but too often it focuses only on what's wrong. *Longe-Vitality* – the art and science of living a long, vital life – is about what's possible. It's about harnessing the science of exercise, nutrition, recovery, and mindset – not just to extend lifespan, but also to expand healthspan. To live long, strong, and well, with a sense of purpose.

Here's how our journey unfolds:

- Chapter 1 introduces Sister Madonna Buder, a living parable of purpose in motion, showing that the river of life can surge with renewed energy at any age.

- Chapter 2 shares the quiet strength of my grand-mothers, whose daily rhythms of care and movement shaped my understanding of graceful ageing.

- Chapters 3 to 7 dig into the science: genes versus environment, heart health, strength, and nutrition. Within these pages, you'll find practical tools and practices, including aerobic training and intermittent walking therapy (IWT), that help slow biological ageing.

- Chapters 8 and 9 explore the soul of movement: the joy, purpose, and resilience that keep us running when the body might otherwise say "stop."

- Chapter 10 reminds us that vitality isn't built in isolation. Community, whether in a local run club or through shared acts of service, fuels our health.

- Finally, chapter 11 explores legacy: how to live well, but also how to leave well, lighting the path for those who follow.

Longe-Vitality isn't about elite athletes, miracle pills, or chasing some impossible fountain of youth. It's about real people, like that 70-year-old woman at the start line beside me, who remind us that vitality has no expiry date. It's about transforming not just how long we live, but how well we live.

Running gave me back my life, turning the Fat Doc into the Run Doc. It reminded me that healing isn't just about avoiding illness; it's about embracing the fullness of who we're meant to be. Through over 10,000 clinical encounters, I've seen the same truth echoed: we have more control than we think.

This is your invitation to step into that truth. To lace up. To move with purpose. To forge a new path for the river of life.

Welcome to *Longe-Vitality*.

Your next great run begins now.

CHAPTER 1

THE RIVER OF LIFE

FLOWING WITH PURPOSE

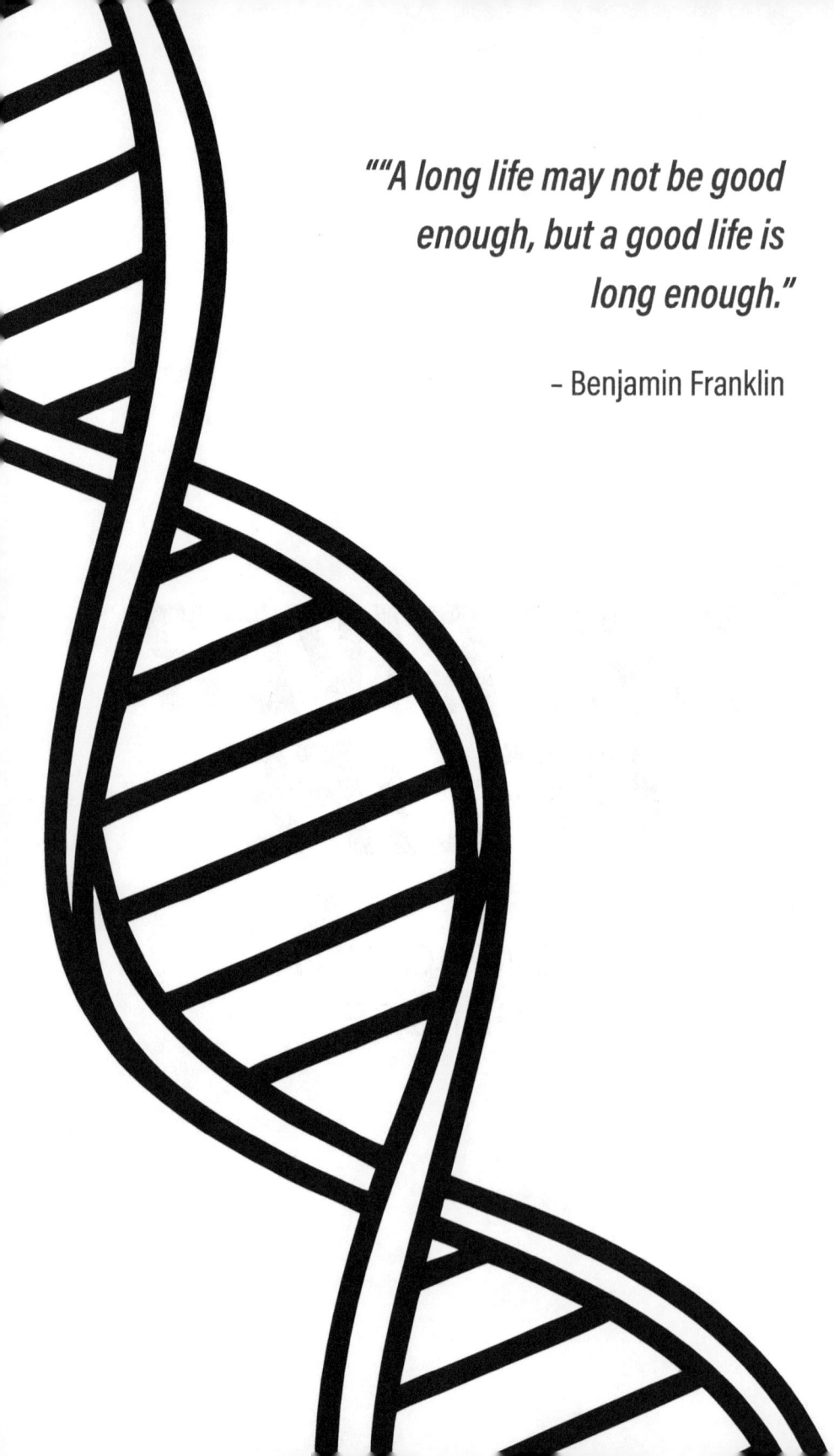

""A long life may not be good enough, but a good life is long enough."

– Benjamin Franklin

LONGE-VITALITY – ALIGNING SCIENCE WITH SOUL

Imagine life as a river, flowing ever forward with energy. In youth, it rushes with excitement and clarity. In midlife, it weaves through rocks, rapids, and sometimes still pools of reflection. And in older age, many believe the river must slow to a trickle or dry up altogether. But must it?

In 2009, the Nobel Prize in Physiology or Medicine was awarded to Elizabeth Blackburn, Carol Greider, and Jack Szostak for their groundbreaking discovery of telomeres, the protective caps at the ends of chromosomes, and the enzyme telomerase, which helps maintain telomere length.[1] Often likened to the plastic tips on shoelaces, telomeres safeguard our genetic material from fraying and instability. Yet, each time our cells divide, these caps shorten, acting as a biological clock of ageing.[2] In the metaphorical River of Life, telomeres are the banks that hold the current steady; as they erode, the river's flow becomes turbulent, leading to cellular decline, disease, and ultimately death.

Three extraordinary individuals – Sister Madonna Buder, Dr Shigeaki Hinohara, and Tao Porchon-Lynch – remind us that the river need not dry. If guided with purpose, it can run clear and strong well into the later decades of life. They show us how to age not just with longevity, but also with vitality and joy – that is, *Longe-Vitality*.

Longe-Vitality isn't about passively drifting downstream,

but about actively shaping the flow through purposeful choices: nourishing food, regular movement, restorative sleep, stress mastery, and meaningful connection, concepts we'll elaborate on as we move through the pages of this book.

The good news? Research suggests that lifestyle factors can slow telomere shortening, even lengthen them, effectively reinforcing the riverbanks. Therefore, by aligning science with soul, we can extend not just lifespan, but also healthspan, the vibrant years in which we thrive, contributing to the world while riding the river with strength, clarity, and joy.

THE IRON NUN: SISTER MADONNA BUDER

Sister Madonna Buder, affectionately known as the 'Iron Nun', is one of the most iconic examples of active ageing in modern times. She began running at 48, the same age I was when I wrote this chapter (and completed my first 100-mile ultramarathon), entering her first triathlon at 52. Late start? Hardly. It was just her beginning. Over the following decades, she completed over 45 Ironman Triathlons and, at age 82, became the oldest woman to finish an Ironman. Now in her 90s, Sister Madonna continues to run, cycle, and inspire.[3]

Her story tells us that the river of life doesn't slow because of age; it slows when we abandon movement and purpose.

Sister Buder continues flowing forward because her movement is powered by meaning. Her triathlons are a form of prayer in motion – not a test of ego, but a celebration of spirit.

THE DOCTOR OF IKIGAI: DR SHIGEAKI HINOHARA

Across the Pacific, in Japan, Dr Shigeaki Hinohara carried his purpose well past his 100th birthday. A practising physician, professor, and author, he worked until the age of 105. He believed that the key to health and longevity isn't just physical; it's having a reason to wake up each morning. In Japanese culture, this is known as *ikigai*: your reason for being.

Dr Hinohara's *ikigai* was to serve others. Even in his centenarian years, he gave lectures, wrote books, and saw patients, rejecting the idea of retirement. He advised people to eat lightly, walk daily, and avoid rigid schedules. Most importantly, he urged everyone to discover what makes their heart sing and pursue it, no matter their age.[4]

He once said, "To stay healthy, always take the stairs and carry your own things. I take two stairs at a time to get my muscles moving."[5] That childlike enthusiasm, for work, for movement, for purpose, kept his river of life flowing energetically until the very end.

THE DANCING YOGI:
TAO PORCHON-LYNCH

Now, let's travel west to the United States to meet Tao Porchon-Lynch, the world's oldest yoga teacher. A former model, dancer, and actress, Tao taught yoga classes well into her 101st year.[6] With painted toenails, bright lipstick, and an infectious laugh, she defied every stereotype of ageing.

"There is nothing you cannot do," she would often tell her students.[7] And she meant it. Tao survived World War II, marched with Gandhi, and founded the Yoga Teachers Association.[8] She didn't just teach poses; she taught the philosophy that joy is a choice and movement is a celebration of life.

Even after a hip replacement in her 90s, Tao returned to competitive ballroom dancing. Her partner? A man less than half her age.[9] Her spirit? Timeless. She taught that your body isn't a barrier. Your thoughts are. Right until the end, her river flowed with grace and sass, refusing to be dammed by age.

DECIPHER THE SCIENCE OF
PURPOSE AND AGEING

The stories of Sister Madonna Buder, Dr Shigeaki Hinohara, and Tao Porchon-Lynch are more than inspiring anecdotes. They align with a growing body of scientific research that's reshaping how we understand ageing.

Let's explore five key areas where science validates the power of purposeful movement.

1. Exercise Delays Biological Ageing

A 2023 study from Loma Linda University found that even brief sessions of high-intensity interval training (HIIT) can significantly reduce biological age in sedentary older adults. Using next-generation measurement techniques, researchers observed that participants who engaged in short bursts of HIIT experienced a reduction in biological age of approximately 3.6 years.[10] Essentially, their cells began functioning as though they belonged to someone nearly 4 years younger.

The study involved 30 sedentary adults, divided into an exercise group and a control group. The exercise group participated in three sessions of HIIT per week for 4 weeks, while the control group maintained their usual routines.[11] The findings suggest that even minimal doses of regular exercise can have a profound impact on slowing the ageing process at the molecular level, underscoring the importance of incorporating regular physical activity into our daily routines, even in small amounts, to promote healthier ageing and potentially extend lifespan.

While Sister Madonna and Tao didn't perform HIIT in a lab, their long sessions of endurance and flexibility training likely produced similar benefits: enhanced mitochondrial health, improved metabolism, and reduced systemic inflammation.

Dr Hinohara, through his daily walking, similarly demonstrated that even regular, low-impact movement keeps biological systems resilient.

2. Strength Training Extends Healthspan

Dr Eric Topol, a renowned cardiologist and founder of the Scripps Research Institute, has dedicated much of his career to studying the factors that contribute to healthy ageing. His research includes exploring the genes associated with healthspan through the analysis of over 1,400 individuals aged 80 and above.[12]

Topol promotes regular physical activity, particularly resistance training, as a key determinant in slowing the biological ageing process. He emphasises that incorporating resistance training into your routine can enhance muscle strength, improve balance, and reduce the risk of chronic diseases. At 70, Topol himself has adopted a strength-training regimen, and for those who can't get to the gym, he recommends starting with home-based exercises, such as planks, squats, push-ups, and lunges to maintain, or even improve, health and vitality.[13]

In his book *Super Agers: An Evidence-Based Approach to Longevity*, Topol provides a comprehensive guide to extending healthspan. He advocates for a holistic approach that includes regular physical activity, a balanced diet, sufficient sleep, and strong social connections. By making these lifestyle adjustments, individuals can potentially add up to a decade of healthy, disease-free life.[14]

Practices like Tao's flowing yoga contribute to building and maintaining the musculoskeletal strength that keeps our bodies functional and youthful.

3. Movement Preserves Brain Function

Running, yoga, and movement practices all protect the ageing brain. A 2024 systematic review titled analysed 9,935 articles and ultimately reviewed 17 rigorous studies. It found that aerobic exercise, especially at higher intensities, boosts cortical excitability, leads to structural brain changes, enhances learning, and improves cognition across diverse age groups and health statuses.[15]

Another 2024 prospective cohort study examined healthy young and middle-aged adults and revealed that regular aerobic exercise elevates levels of brain-derived neurotrophic factor (BDNF) and glial cell-derived neurotrophic factor (GDNF) in the blood. These neurotrophic factors are crucial for supporting neuroplasticity and are linked to better cognitive function and reduced depressive symptoms.[16]

Together, these studies underscore how aerobic activity

fosters neuroplasticity by enhancing neurotrophic support and inducing functional and structural brain adaptations, thereby helping to delay cognitive decline and bolster mental resilience in both young and older adults.

Meditation in motion, be it Tao's yoga, Sister Madonna's running, or Dr Hinohara's walking, encourages brain-body harmony. Dr Hinohara wrote until his final year, his regular physical activity and social engagement serving as cognitive training that rivalled common mental exercises, such as completing crossword puzzles.[17]

4. Purpose Predicts Health Outcomes

One of the most cited findings from the Blue Zones research, led by National Geographic Fellow Dan Buettner, is the strong link between a sense of purpose and longevity. Blue Zones are locations around the world with higher-than-average concentrations of centenarians.

In Okinawa, Japan, home to one of the world's highest concentrations of centenarians, many residents follow the *ikigai* (reason for being) philosophy. Researchers surveyed older adults and found that those who can clearly articulate their *ikigai* not only live longer but also enjoy better physical and mental health. The findings indicate that having a purpose may reduce chronic stress, encourage healthy behaviours, and keep individuals socially and mentally engaged, key ingredients for a long life.[18] Overall, purpose appears to act as a protective factor, reducing the risk of cardiovascular disease and, in turn, increasing lifespan. Interestingly, the *ikigai* effect still holds even after accounting for factors such as diet, exercise, and social support.[19] Similar trends were observed in other Blue Zones, including Nicoya in Costa Rica, where the term *plan de vida* captures a comparable idea.[20]

The Blue Zones study highlights that while nutrition and lifestyle matter greatly, waking up each day with a reason to live may be one of the most powerful longevity tools available, something accessible to everyone, regardless of age or geography. It's not just what you do; it's why you do it. All three icons of *Longe-Vitality*: Sister Madonna, Tao, and Dr Hinohara, woke each day with purpose. That may be their greatest secret.

5. Consistency Trumps Intensity

A growing body of research supports the principle of consistency over intensity as a key factor in achieving long-term health and longevity. Regular, moderate physical activity, such as brisk walking, cycling, or light jogging, has been shown to reduce the risk of chronic diseases, improve cardiovascular health, and promote healthy ageing. Studies indicate that people who engage in daily moderate exercise accumulate greater lifetime health benefits compared to those who perform sporadic high-intensity workouts but remain otherwise sedentary. Consistency allows for sustainable habits, reducing the risk of injury and burnout often associated with intense, intermittent training.

For example, the Copenhagen City Heart Study found that moderate joggers have significantly lower mortality rates than both sedentary individuals and those engaging in strenuous jogging.[21] Likewise, research from the Harvard Alumni Health Study demonstrated that regular moderate activity in midlife predicts better physical function decades later.[22]

Longevity experts highlight that daily, manageable exercise supports metabolic health, lowers inflammation, and sustains mental wellbeing – benefits that compound over time.[23] The key takeaway is that maintaining a regular, enjoyable activity routine is more effective for healthspan than chasing sporadic extremes. Tao practised yoga every day. Dr Hinohara avoided rigid regimens but embraced daily routines. Sister Madonna made training a lifestyle.

Like water flowing over stone, steady habits shape long-term health.

THE SOUL OF MOVEMENT

When we move with purpose, we do more than maintain our health – we nourish the soul. Movement becomes more than a physical act; it transforms into a form of self-expression, connection, and meaning. A morning run along a quiet trail, a mindful yoga flow, or a walk with a friend can ground us in the present moment, reminding us of our place in the world. Purposeful movement taps into our innate human need for rhythm and flow, engaging not just muscles, but also heart and mind. It can be an act of gratitude for the body we inhabit, a celebration of life's capacity for growth and change. Across cultures, movement has always been tied to ritual, storytelling, and spiritual practice, from Indigenous dance ceremonies to pilgrimages spanning hundreds of kilometres.

Modern science now affirms what ancient traditions knew: movement fosters mental clarity, emotional balance, and a deeper sense of connection to ourselves and others. When driven by intention rather than mere obligation, it cultivates joy, resilience, and hope. Ultimately, the soul of movement lies in its ability to unify body and spirit, turning each step, stretch, or stride into a testament to the simple truth: we were born to move, with purpose.

Sister Madonna sees her running as a form of prayer. Tao saw her yoga as a dance of spirit. Dr Hinohara treated medicine as a calling. None of them saw age as an excuse to stop.

They saw it as a reason to start anew: to go deeper, to serve more, to celebrate life while it's still flowing.

This is the soul of *Longe-Vitality*: movement infused with meaning. It's not about beating the clock. It's about feeling alive in your body, awake in your mind, and aligned with your deeper values.

THE RIVER FLOWS ON

The river's current is steady, sometimes gentle, sometimes fierce, yet always moving forward. In life, we're much like that river, constantly flowing through seasons of calm and turbulence. Purpose is the river's channel, the unseen guide shaping its course. Without it, the water may spread aimlessly, losing direction and strength. But when guided by purpose, the river doesn't merely flow; it deepens. Each bend, each tributary, each obstacle becomes a chance to carve a richer path. Purpose gives meaning to the miles we travel, just as the river's destination gives meaning to its journey.

In times of drought, when energy wanes or hope feels thin, purpose keeps the current alive, drawing from hidden springs of resilience. In times of flood, when challenges overwhelm, purpose keeps the river from breaking its banks, channelling that force towards growth and renewal. A purposeful life isn't about rushing to the sea; it's about deepening along the way, nourishing the landscapes we pass, leaving vibrant life in our wake.

The river runs on, unchanged in its movement yet transformed by its depth. And so do we, when every step, every choice, and every breath flows towards something greater than ourselves, our telomeres being preserved with each step towards *Longe-Vitality*.

The lives of Sister Madonna Buder, Tao Porchon-Lynch, and Dr Shigeaki Hinohara show us that ageing isn't a dry decline, but a rich, flowing chapter of life. Each of these inspiring people chose to keep moving, keep giving, and keep seeking joy, and the river rewarded them.

You're not too late to improve the flow of your river. In fact, you're right on time.

RUN DOC'S LONGE-VITALITY TIPS

1

Start where you are.
Whether you're 25 or 85, today is a perfect day to begin.
Walk, stretch, dance, run. The type of movement matters
less than the commitment to move.

2

Train for life, not for finish lines.
Adopt the athlete's mindset: move regularly, eat mindfully,
sleep deeply. Fitness isn't just for competition – it's for
participation in life.

3

Discover your *ikigai*.
What gives your life meaning? Helping others? Creating
art? Being present with loved ones? Let your purpose
shape your daily rhythm – because purpose is the
ultimate performance enhancer.

4

Build the habit of movement.
Five minutes per day is enough to start. Then five
becomes ten. Ten becomes thirty. Consistency turns
routine into ritual – until movement feels as natural as
breathing.

5

Let movement be joyful.
Don't punish your body – celebrate it. Tao danced
with delight. Sister Madonna smiles through miles. Dr
Hinohara walked with wonder. Find your own rhythm –
and move through life with joy.

LET PURPOSE PROPEL YOU FORWARD

The river of life flows onward. It invites you in, not to paddle against the current of age, but to glide with purpose. Whether you're lacing up for your first walk, your 50th marathon, or teaching yoga at 101, you're part of this movement. So breathe deeply. Step forward. Let your life, like the river, move with strength, with grace, and above all, with purpose.

CHAPTER 2

ROOTS OF LONGEVITY

A TALE OF TWO

"The secret of longevity is to keep breathing, but the root of living long and well lies in eating lightly, moving daily, loving deeply, and worrying less"

– Anonymous (Modern Wisdom)

THE QUIET POWER OF ORDINARY DAYS

In a world fascinated by breakthroughs in biotechnology, supplements, and the quantified self, the most enduring lessons on longevity often emerge not from a laboratory but from the quiet routines of ordinary people living with extraordinary grace. This chapter is an ode to such lives, those lived with humility, resilience, and purpose. It explores the legacies of two remarkable women from my own lineage: my paternal grandmother, FC Wong (*Ma-Ma*), and my maternal grandmother, SL Wong (*Por-Por*), whose gentle, habitual rhythms were as instructive as any modern health protocol.

In their own modest ways, their lives mirrored those of longevity icons like Emma Morano, the Italian supercentenarian who lived to 117 by honouring routine, resilience, and family ties, and Sarah Ntiro, a Ugandan grandmother, educator, and human rights advocate who remained actively engaged in community well into her twilight years. These women, from different cultures and continents, shared a common thread: a life lived with deep purpose, sustained movement, and an abiding connection to those around them.

FC WONG: THE MORNING WALKER OF CAUSEWAY BAY

My grandmother, FC Wong, was living proof of the principle 'consistency over intensity' (described in chapter one) long before it was popularised in scientific journals. Every morning before the sun crested Hong Kong's skyline, she laced up her shoes and stepped into the terraced maze of the Mid-Levels district, or made her way to the idyllic harbour-side Causeway Bay region of Victoria Park. With a modest gait but unmistakable determination, she walked with a small posse of 'hiking' friends: older women who shared stories, laughter, and the city's steep inclines. I recall two anecdotes from my childhood memory.

Anecdote One – the Rainy-Day Pact

One drizzly winter morning, my grandmother's friends suggested skipping the walk and meeting directly at Yum Cha in Causeway Bay, where their walks often concluded. *Ma-Ma* shook her head, handed out plastic ponchos, and said, "If we only walk when the weather is perfect, we won't walk for half the year" (she was exaggerating, but monsoon season does happen and often lasts for days!).

They set out under grey skies, splashing through puddles, laughing at the absurdity of their soggy shoes. That morning became one of their most memorable outings, a reminder that resilience comes from showing up, not from waiting for perfect conditions.

Anecdote Two – the Steeper Path

In the path up Wan Chai Gap Road, there was a choice between a flatter loop and a steeper route up a small hill. Many mornings, especially when the group was feeling tired, the flat loop was the default. But my grandmother had a mischievous streak. "We're already here," she would say with a grin, "why not climb a little?" By the time they reached the top, the city's harbour stretched below them like a living postcard. *Ma-Ma* knew that small, repeated challenges kept both the body and spirit sharp.

Science Behind FC Wong's Longe-Vitality

Once they arrived at Yum Cha each morning, *Ma-Ma* would savour jasmine tea and dim sum staples: *har gow, siu mai,* and *cheung fun.* The familiarity of the walk, the nourishment of food, and the intimacy of friendship formed a kind of sacred daily liturgy. Science now affirms what my grandmother knew intuitively: longevity is built on the foundation of small, repeated acts of care for one's body and soul.

What might appear mundane was, in fact, profoundly protective. According to a 2021 study, daily walking, particularly in the range of 7,000 to 9,000 steps, correlates with a significant reduction in all-cause mortality.[1] FC's habit, repeated over decades, wasn't a fitness fad but a philosophy of life – movement not for performance, but for presence.

And then there was her tea. The simple act of sipping jasmine tea daily was more than cultural; it was medicinal. One prospective cohort study, which included over 100,000 Chinese adults, found that habitual tea drinkers (those who consume tea three or more times per week) live on average 1.26 years longer than non-habitual tea drinkers (those who consume tea fewer than three times per week). The study also found that habitual tea drinking was associated with significantly lower rates of atherosclerotic cardiovascular disease (ASCVD), ASCVD mortality, and all-cause mortality. Rich in polyphenols, tea supports cardiovascular health, reduces inflammation, and bolsters mental clarity, factors crucial to healthy ageing.[2]

But perhaps the greatest elixir was the laughter and connection FC shared during those walks and tea sessions. Research consistently shows that social engagement protects against depression, cognitive decline, and chronic disease. For example, a 2024 longitudinal study found that social connection and engagement are consistently associated with fewer depressive symptoms, both before and after a cancer diagnosis, highlighting the buffering impact of social ties during times of stress.[3] Further, a 2022 meta-analysis found that poor social relationships – with friends, family, or other sources of socialisation or emotional support – are significantly associated with cognitive decline.[4] Finally, a cross-sectional study of older adults with chronic illness found that higher perceived social support significantly mediates the negative impact of perceived burdensomeness on psychological wellbeing, showing how social support buffers mental health challenges when navigating chronic disease.[5]

FC didn't seek longevity; she simply lived fully, and in doing so, laid the foundation for a longer, more vital life.

SL WONG: THE RESILIENT MATRIARCH

While FC epitomised graceful movement, SL Wong was a pillar of strength and perseverance. A mother of six and wartime performer, *Por-Por* lived a life that reflected quiet heroism. During World War II, she performed Chinese opera to uplift soldiers' spirits, a vivid example of how social engagement in the form of art and shared cultural experience can fortify morale during hardship. The camaraderie backstage, the shared meals after performances, and the applause from weary audiences all served as a protective balm against despair in turbulent times.

Anecdote One – Opera in the Dark

One evening, during an air raid, the theatre lights failed. Rather than abandon the performance, *Por-Por* and her troupe lit oil lamps and continued singing. Soldiers and civilians huddled together, listening in the dim glow. That night, art wasn't just entertainment; it was medicine for the spirit, a shared act of resilience.

Anecdote Two – the Western Market Ascent

Into her 70s and beyond, *Por-Por* would walk, groceries in hand, up the steep slopes from Western Market to her Mid-Levels home. Along the way, she greeted neighbours, exchanged recipes, and paused to chat with stallholders. These small but regular connections kept her woven into the fabric of her community, protecting her from the social isolation that can hasten cognitive and physical decline.

Anecdote Three – The Mahjong Table

Every Sunday, *Por-Por* hosted a mahjong game that drew family, friends, and neighbours. The tiles clicked rhythmically, punctuated by teasing remarks and shared snacks. Beyond the game itself, the gathering was a ritual of belonging, a place where stories were told, problems were shared, and laughter was guaranteed. The mental stimulation of strategy combined with the emotional nourishment of companionship made it a quiet, weekly defence against loneliness and age-related decline.

Science Behind SL Wong's Longe-Vitality

In her own way, SL Wong demonstrated what modern research confirms: sustained social engagement – whether through shared purpose, casual encounters, or structured gatherings – acts as a powerful safeguard for mental and physical health.

Additionally, she had unwittingly become her own strength trainer. According to a 2022 meta-analysis, older adults who perform weight-bearing activities, such as carrying heavy groceries, have better muscle mass, bone density, and lower risk of falls. The study examined the effects of progressive resistance training (PRT) on muscle strength and bone mineral density (BMD). Analysing data from numerous high-quality trials, the authors found that PRT, especially when combined with weight-bearing or impact-loading exercises, such as stair climbing, brisk walking, or jumping, significantly improves lower-limb muscle strength and increases BMD at key fracture-prone sites, including the hip and femoral neck. These physiological benefits translate into a lower risk of falls and fractures, two of the most serious threats to independence in older age. The review also highlights that training programs must be performed at sufficient intensity, with gradual progression, to achieve optimal results. Importantly, the authors concluded that well-designed PRT programs are both safe and effective for older populations, supporting their widespread use as a preventive strategy against age-related musculoskeletal decline.[6]

SL needed no gym membership. Her gym was the city, and her weights were the necessities of daily life. Yet SL's most enduring act of longevity wasn't physical; it was emotional. She was the primary carer for her youngest grandson from birth until his teenage years. That constant, loving presence – structured, dependable, and sacrificial – was her legacy.

As we know, people who report having a strong sense of purpose in life (or *ikigai*) show reduced risk of chronic illness and early death. A large 2019 cohort study, which analysed nearly 7,000 participants over age 50, confirmed that individuals with a higher purpose-in-life score experience significantly lower all-cause mortality and reduced risk of death from cardiovascular and circulatory conditions.[7] Another 2019 study, which included over 9,700 adults, found that people with higher affective wellbeing – defined as enjoyment of life and absence of depressive symptoms – experience longer life expectancy and healthspan, living free of chronic disease and disability longer than those with lower wellbeing scores.[8]

Purpose doesn't need to be grand. For SL, it was wrapped in making school lunches, facilitating early morning wake-ups, and providing a warm hand to hold in times of need. Through her caregiving, remaining useful and connecting well into her later years, she aged with grace.

INTERGENERATIONAL ECHOES: EMMA MORANO AND SARAH NTIRO

From my two grandmothers, FC Wong and SL Wong, to global longevity figures like Emma Morano and Sarah Ntiro, one fact remains the same: each of these inspiring women, whether knowingly or not, adopted practices that science now tells us are the keys to *Longe-Vitality*.

Emma Morano, born in 1899 in Civiasco, Italy, lived to an extraordinary 117 years and 137 days, becoming one of the world's oldest verified people. Her longevity was anchored in simple, consistent habits, including going to bed and waking early and eating a straightforward diet.[9] "I eat two eggs a day, and that's it," she famously remarked, reflecting her belief in moderation and routine.[10] She often attributed her resilience to her independence, which she gained after escaping an abusive marriage.[11]

Emma's steady lifestyle mirrors findings from longevity studies in other regions, where caloric restriction is associated with healthy ageing.[12] In an age where many seek elaborate anti-ageing interventions, her story offers a timeless reminder: the foundations of long life often lie in simplicity and consistency.

Sarah Ntiro is another longevity icon. Born in Uganda, she was a remarkable trailblazer for women's education and the first woman from East Africa to graduate from Oxford University. Her early life was marked by barriers, both colonial and cultural, that sought to limit women's roles to the domestic sphere. Yet Sarah defied these constraints, returning home to dedicate her career to teaching, curriculum development, and mentoring generations of young women. Her advocacy extended far beyond the classroom: she was a vocal proponent of gender equity in education, often challenging policymakers and traditional norms with a quiet yet unshakeable conviction.[13] Her resilience was forged in hardship, yet her instinctive response was service – a lifetime commitment to lifting others. In her, we see a vivid truth: purposeful engagement in community life sustains not only the individual spirit but also the collective wellbeing.

Sarah Ntiro taught us that purposeful living doesn't retire with age. Instead, it transforms into mentoring roles, community engagement, storytelling, and quiet leadership. Her life, like SL Wong's, reveals how the role of elder is one of profound societal value.

THE SCIENCE OF QUIET RESILIENCE

Let's now re-examine the science of quiet resilience and its associated Longe-Vitality.

1. Physical Activity

Daily movement, even in modest forms such as walking, climbing stairs, or lifting groceries, is a cornerstone of healthy ageing and disease prevention. Regular physical activity supports cardiovascular function by improving circulation, lowering blood pressure, and enhancing heart efficiency. It also helps maintain muscle mass and bone density, reducing the risk of frailty and falls in later life. From a mental health perspective, movement stimulates the release of endorphins, alleviates symptoms of anxiety and depression, and promotes better cognitive function.

The World Health Organization (WHO) recommends at least 150 minutes of moderate-intensity aerobic exercise per week for adults, combined with muscle-strengthening activities on two or more days.[14] However, research shows that even smaller amounts, when performed consistently, can deliver meaningful benefits.[15] For example, short bouts of walking integrated throughout the day can lower all-cause mortality risk, while light resistance training preserves mobility and independence in older adults. The key lies not in intensity alone, but in sustained, regular participation, turning movement into a lifelong habit.

2. Social Connection

Harvard's landmark Study of Adult Development, one of the longest-running studies of adult life, has shown that close relationships – more than wealth, social status, or fame – are the strongest predictors of long-term happiness and health. The research, spanning over 80 years, found that people who are more socially connected to family, friends, and community live longer, experience less chronic illness, and maintain sharper mental faculties as they age. Loneliness, on the other hand, is linked to poorer health, faster cognitive decline, and shorter lifespans.[16]

3. Purpose in Life

Purpose both propels us forward along the river of life and keeps us afloat. Not only that, but having a sense of purpose is associated with a 15 percent lower risk of death.[17] Purpose isn't just about having goals; it's about being needed. Ultimately, it gives structure to life and buffers against stress and illness.

4. Nutrition and Ritual

For many, including my grandmothers, eating isn't just about caloric intake; it's also about the sensory and social experience – savouring flavours, sharing stories, and strengthening bonds.

Modern research supports what my grandmothers' lives illustrated: eating mindfully and socially is linked to better digestion, lower stress, and improved long-term health outcomes.[18] Additionally, shared meals promote healthier food choices, reduce loneliness, and enhance psychological wellbeing, all of which contribute to longevity.[19] Moreover, traditional diets rich in whole foods with minimal processing are associated with reduced chronic disease risk.[20]

RUN DOC'S LONGE-VITALITY TIPS

1

Walk daily – find joy in every step.
Aim for 7,000 to 10,000 steps each day. Walk through places that lift your spirit – a quiet park, a coastal path, or even the rhythmic city streets. The goal isn't just distance; it's delight.

2

Drink tea with intention.
Savour each sip of green, jasmine, or oolong tea. These antioxidant-rich brews calm inflammation, support your heart, and centre your mind – a mindful pause in a hurried world.

3

Lift something heavy.
Strength is youth preserved. Whether it's carrying groceries, using resistance bands, or doing bodyweight exercises, lifting builds bones, boosts metabolism, and keeps independence within reach.

4

Cultivate connection.
Healthy ageing isn't solitary. Share meals, stories, and laughter with family, neighbours, and your wider community. Connection strengthens both immunity and joy.

5

Live with purpose.
Purpose is the ultimate longevity medicine. Care for a grandchild, mentor a student, volunteer for a cause, or simply show up wholeheartedly for those you love. When your life ripples outward, vitality flows inward.

LEGACIES IN MOTION

My grandmothers didn't set out to become examples of longevity. They simply lived, with conviction, compassion, and quiet courage. Their lives echo the enduring wisdom of Emma Morano, who believed in simplicity and family, and Sarah Ntiro, who embodied purposeful engagement well into old age.

Longevity isn't a product to be bought. It's cultivated on footpaths, in kitchens, tea shops, grocery stalls, and the hearts of those who show up daily for others. It's found not in perfect health, but in resilient spirits, and it lives on in the habits we inherit, the stories we tell, and the people we choose to become.

To walk in their footsteps isn't to chase time, but to honour it.

CHAPTER 3

THE LONGEVITY BLUEPRINT

GENES VS. ENVIRONMENT

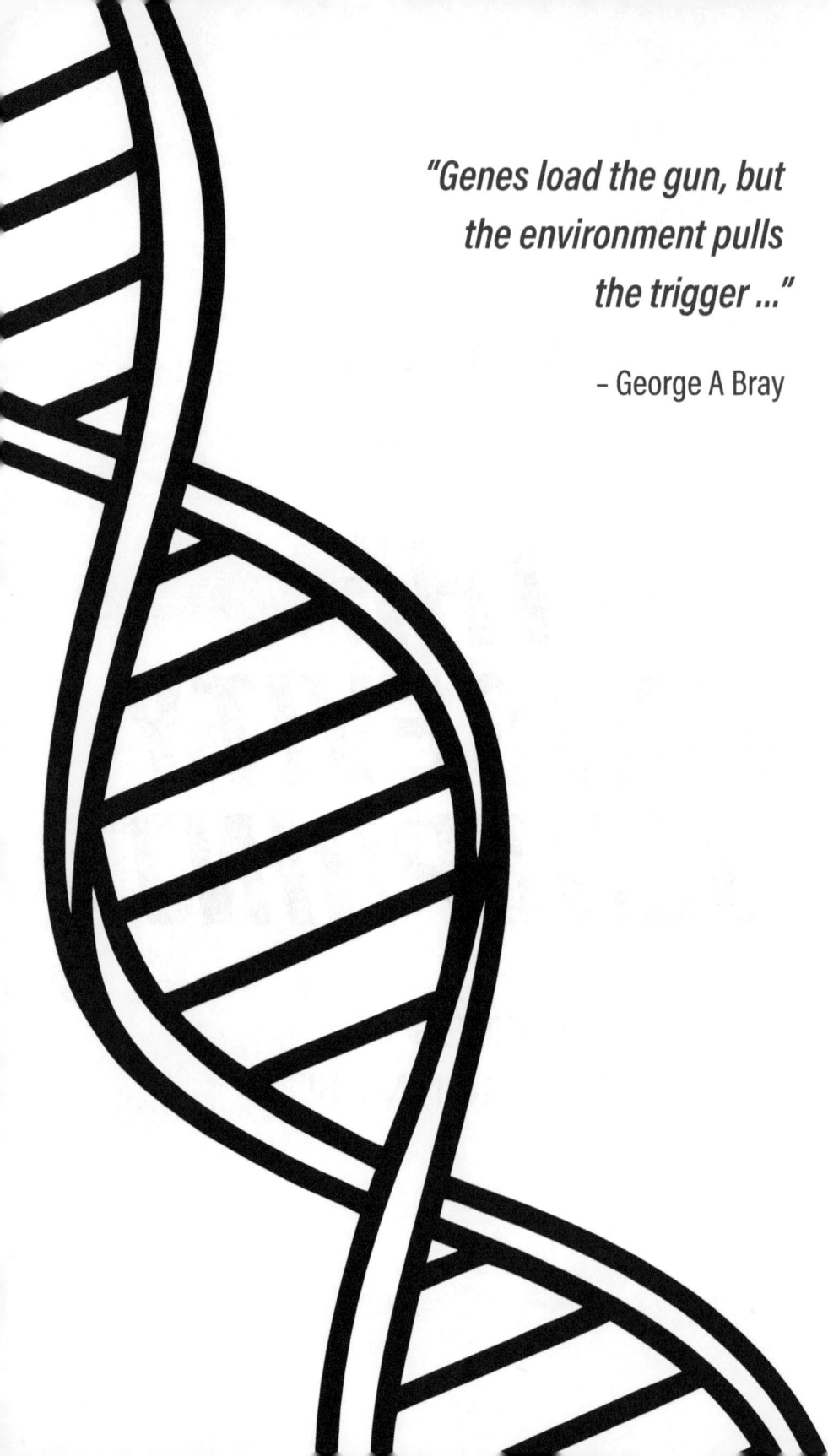

"Genes load the gun, but the environment pulls the trigger ..."

– George A Bray

REWRITING THE NARRATIVE OF AGEING

Ageing isn't a disease. It's not a punishment for surviving into the future. Yet in modern society, we too often view it through the lens of decline and loss, of fading energy, failing memory, and fragility. The 'anti-ageing' industry is a billion-dollar behemoth built on the idea that ageing is something to fight. But around the world, and even within our own families and communities, we encounter living proof that ageing can be vibrant, joyful, and purpose-filled.

So what separates those who flourish in their later years from those who merely endure them? Is it simply a genetic gift, lucky DNA, or is there something more within our influence?

Science has spoken. While genetics lay the foundation, it's lifestyle and environment – the choices we make and the conditions we create – that build the house of longevity.

THE GENETIC BASELINE:
JUST A STARTING LINE

The question of how much our genes determine our lifespan has been studied for decades. One of the most cited studies on the role of genetics in longevity comes from Denmark, where in 1996 researchers analysed the lifespans of 2,872 identical and fraternal twin pairs. By comparing lifespan similarity between genetically identical twins and those sharing only half their genes, the researchers were able to tease apart the influence of heredity from environmental and lifestyle factors. Their conclusion was striking: only about 25 percent of the variability in human lifespan can be attributed to genetic factors, while the remaining 75 percent is shaped by non-genetic influences such as diet, physical activity, social connections, mental health, and exposure to environmental risks.[1]

More recent genomic research has trimmed this estimate further. In 2018, leveraging data from *Ancestry*, researchers isolated the heritable components of longevity from environmental influences. The findings were even more striking than earlier twin studies: the genetic contribution to lifespan was estimated to be only around 7 percent, suggesting that the vast majority of variation in how long people live is explained by lifestyle, environmental exposures, socio-economic factors, and chance.[2]

Even though genes aren't the primary factor in determining lifespan, we shouldn't totally discount our genetics. In 2019, researchers conducted one of the largest genome-wide association studies (GWAS) to date, analysing genetic and health data from over one million individuals to better understand the biological determinants of human lifespan. Rather than studying lifespan directly in participants, researchers examined the lifespans of their parents, allowing for a powerful proxy measure while minimising biases linked to environmental exposures. The study identified several genetic variants associated with longevity, many of which were located in pathways related to cardiovascular health, immune function, and lipid metabolism.[3] These findings reinforce the concept that common diseases such as coronary artery disease and type 2 diabetes significantly influence lifespan, and genetic predispositions to these conditions may partially explain differences in survival. Importantly, the research suggests that lifespan is a polygenic trait – shaped by the combined effect of many small genetic contributions – rather than the result of a few major 'longevity genes'. The study also highlights the importance of modifiable risk factors: while genes play a role, lifestyle choices, disease prevention, and healthy ageing practices remain critical in determining overall healthspan and lifespan.

The implication of the research is clear: while our genes can offer a slight advantage or disadvantage, the overwhelming determinants of healthy ageing and longevity lie in modifiable lifestyle and environmental factors. In other words, up to 90 percent of our longevity isn't inherited, but cultivated. Genes set the potential, but they're not destiny. What we eat, how we move, the quality of our relationships, and how we respond to life's challenges all hold far greater sway over our lifespan than our DNA alone. Therefore, every day offers a new opportunity to invest in a longer, healthier, and more vibrant life.

JEANNE CALMENT: LIVING BEYOND HER GENES

The story of Frenchwoman Jeanne Calment, verified as the oldest person in recorded history, provides a striking illustration of the fact that lifestyle and environment can outweigh genetics when it comes to determining longevity. Jeanne lived to the remarkable age of 122 years and 164 days, passing away in 1997. Interestingly, old age didn't run in her family. While her parents lived into their 80s and 90s, a respectable lifespan, it was nowhere near Jeanne's record.[4] She was an exception, suggesting that the secret to her longevity was less about DNA and more about the way she lived.

Calment's daily life was a tapestry woven with movement, moderation, and joy. She rode her bicycle until the age of 100, lived independently until she was well past 110, and continued to walk with minimal assistance into her final years. Her diet was far from disciplined. She enjoyed olive oil, chocolate, and wine, and famously smoked a cigarette or two each day until nearly 117.[5] Yet these indulgences were balanced by an overall moderate approach, never falling into excess.

Perhaps Jeanne's most remarkable trait was her resilience to stress. Jean-Marie Robine, a researcher who co-authored *The Longest Life: 122 Extraordinary Years of Jeanne Calment – from Van Gogh's Time to Ours*, described her as someone who "constitutionally and biologically speaking, was immune to stress," a quality now recognised as beneficial for health and longevity.[6] Jeanne also had an active social life, and as we know, social connection is an important pillar of longevity.[7] Essentially, her lifestyle was the perfect recipe for a long and happy life.

From a scientific perspective, Jeanne's life underscores three important insights:

1. Genes aren't destiny – large-scale studies show that genetics may account for only 7 to 25 percent of lifespan variability.[8]

2. Social connection matters – modern research confirms that strong social engagement protects against depression, cognitive decline, and chronic disease, all of which influence mortality.[9]

3. Psychological resilience is powerful – emotional stability, optimism, and low reactivity to stress are associated with lower inflammation, better immune function, and improved cardiovascular health.[10]

Jeanne's story isn't an argument for replicating her exact habits – few would recommend smoking at any age – but rather it's a demonstration that the overall environment, mindset, and lifestyle can profoundly shape the trajectory of ageing. She moved daily, maintained purpose and relationships, lived with humour, and avoided chronic stress.

In essence, Jeanne Calment lived long not because of what she was born with, but because of how she lived. Her example suggests that, while we can't control the genetic cards we're dealt, we have significant influence over how we play them.

THE POWER 9: LESSONS FROM THE WORLD'S LONGEST-LIVING PEOPLE

To understand the broader implications of how environment shapes longevity, we once again turn to Blue Zones researcher Dan Buettner. Buettner's landmark research revealed a set of nine lifestyle patterns that transcend geography and culture, offering a blueprint for living longer and better.[11]

1. Natural Movement Throughout the Day

Instead of structured gym sessions, Blue Zone residents integrate activity into daily life, gardening, walking to visit neighbours, tending livestock. Essentially, movement is habitual, not forced.

2. Strong Sense of Purpose

Purpose (*ikigai* in Okinawa and *plan de vida* in Nicoya) sustains resilience and encourages healthier life choices over decades. Essentially, it gives us a reason to get out of bed each day.

3. Stress-Shedding Rituals

Chronic stress accelerates cellular ageing through inflammation and telomere shortening.[12] From Okinawan ancestor veneration to Sardinian afternoon naps, each Blue Zone community has built-in ways to decompress. These rituals are like a daily 'reset button'.

4. 80 Percent Rule

The Okinawan philosophy of *hara hachi bu* means only eating until your stomach is 80 percent full. Many Blue Zone residents eat their last and smallest meal late in the day, fasting until morning and receiving the benefits of caloric restriction.

5. Plant-Based Diet

For many Blue Zone residents, legumes, vegetables, whole grains, and nuts form the dietary core. Meat is eaten sparingly – often only on special occasions. In Loma Linda, California, Seventh-day Adventists thrive on a vegetarian diet rich in beans, nuts, and fruit, which is associated with lower cardiovascular risk.[13]

6. Moderate, Regular Consumption of Wine

In Sardinia and Ikaria, residents often enjoy a glass of locally made wine, rich in polyphenols and consumed socially, with meals. Moderate wine intake, especially in Mediterranean diets, is linked with reduced cardiovascular mortality – though only when combined with an otherwise healthy lifestyle.[14]

7. Belonging to a Faith-Based Community

Attending religious services, regardless of denomination, is a common thread in the lives of Blue Zone residents. Belonging to a faith-based community is associated with an additional 4 to 14 years of life expectancy.[15] The benefits come not just from spiritual practice, but also from social support and shared values.

8. Prioritising Family

In Blue Zones, elders often live with or near their children and grandchildren. Family loyalty ensures care in later life and provides emotional stability, leading to better health outcomes, including protection against depression and dementia.[16]

9. Social Networks That Support Healthy Behaviours

Okinawans form *moais*, lifelong friendship groups that provide mutual support. Positive social ties buffer against illness, encourage good habits, and reduce mortality risk by up to 50 percent.[17] That's right – who you spend time with influences how long you live.

The True Power of the Power 9

It's not one habit alone that's powerful – it's the synergy of all nine. The beauty? None of these habits involve advanced medicine, genetic engineering, or expensive interventions. They're simple and repeatable. They're environmental and behavioural. And they can add decades to your life.

The lesson? Our postcode may matter more than our genetic code, but our daily decisions matter most.

THE GRANDMOTHERS' BLUEPRINT: *POR-POR* AND *MA-MA*

The principles of longevity aren't confined to distant islands or research labs. They're alive in the ordinary lives of extraordinary elders, like my grandmothers.

Por-Por raised seven children during wartime and economic hardship. Yet well into her 90s, she walked to the markets, chopped vegetables with precision, and engaged in multigenerational caregiving with grace. She didn't lift weights, but she carried the emotional, and often the physical, load of a village.

Ma-Ma, by contrast, was a social catalyst. She walked door-to-door to check on friends. She hosted gatherings, led mahjong groups, and was always dressed for visitors. Her faith was strong, her calendar full, and her heart open.

They moved daily, stayed socially engaged, and lived with purpose. Neither wore a fitness tracker. But both embodied *Longe-Vitality*.

RUN DOC RUNDOWN OF THE LIFESTYLE VS. GENETICS DEBATE

Through my research and professional experience as a physician, several longevity facts have become clear.

- **Lifestyle can overcome most genetic risk.**
  As the Run Doc, I've seen it time and again: your DNA may set the opening scene, but your daily choices write the rest of the script. Lifestyle can overcome most genetic risk because movement, nutrition, recovery, mindset, and connection all act like biological 'switches' that turn protective genes on and silence harmful ones. I've run alongside people who came from families riddled with heart disease, diabetes, or dementia, yet through consistent training, balanced eating, and stress management, they've outpaced their genetic odds. To paraphrase obesity researcher George A Bray, your genes may load the gun, but it's

your lifestyle that decides whether or not the trigger is pulled.

- **Movement matters more than your DNA.**
Daily movement, not just occasional exercise, is true magic. Whether it's running a marathon, walking to the shops, or stretching before bed, each step or movement sends a powerful signal to your body: I'm alive, keep me strong. Don't wait for perfect conditions – move today, move daily, and let your body rewrite its own destiny.

- **Purpose changes your biology.**
Purpose-driven activity and social connection lead to healthier ageing. What gets you out of bed in the morning? What's your *ikigai*? Let it be your fuel and your antidote to unhealthy ageing.

Ultimately, the river of life, on its path to *Longe-Vitality*, runs through our choices, not our genes. What choices will you make moving forward?

THE NIGHT SHIFT OF *LONGE-VITALITY*

In the symphony of *Longe-Vitality*, sleep is the silent conductor, working behind the scenes each night to repair, regulate, and rejuvenate. For years, sleep was undervalued: squeezed between work obligations, digital distractions, and the glorification of hustle culture. But the latest science is clear: high-quality, consistent sleep isn't just rest; it's regeneration.

Studies have found a compelling link between optimal sleep (7 to 8 hours per night) and reduced risk of cognitive decline.[18] Why? During deep sleep, the brain activates its glymphatic system: a kind of nightly rinse cycle that clears out beta-amyloid and other metabolic waste that accumulate during wakefulness. This brain-cleaning process appears essential in delaying or preventing neurodegenerative diseases.

On the cellular level, a 2023 study showed that poor sleep, whether due to short duration or frequent interruptions, is associated with shorter telomeres.[19] Simply put, poor sleep may accelerate the ticking of our cellular clock.

Yet, sleep isn't a one-way miracle. It is a double-edged sword. As I've observed in clinical practice, a subset of clients, particularly those who report sleeping more than 12 hours daily (including extra daytime naps), tend to experience worse health outcomes, including persistent fatigue, poor mental health, and reduced physical performance. This aligns with research that has revealed a U-shaped relationship between sleep duration and mortality. Both insufficient and excessive sleep are associated with increased risk of cardiovascular disease, depression, and premature death.[20]

Sleep, like training or nutrition, requires balance. Too little, and the body breaks down. Too much, and vitality dims. It's not just the quantity, but the quality, rhythm, and consistency of sleep that matter. Deep sleep supports tissue repair and growth hormone release, especially critical for older adults seeking to preserve strength and resilience.

The takeaway? Sleep wisely.

LONGEVITY ISN'T JUST YEARS, IT'S ENERGY

We don't pursue *Longe-Vitality* simply to live longer; we pursue it to live better. What good is an extra decade if it's spent in a wheelchair you didn't need to be in, trapped in a house because of lost mobility, or unable to recognise loved ones through the fog of cognitive decline?

The true aim isn't just to extend lifespan, but to expand healthspan, the years we live with independence, mental clarity, physical strength, and joy. A long life without these qualities is merely existence; a long life with them is a gift.

Sister Madonna Buder wakes at dawn not because she's driven by fear of ageing, but because she's energised by the day ahead. She runs not to cling to youth, but to honour life, each step a prayer of gratitude, each race a celebration of what her body can still do. She is living proof that it's possible to grow older without giving in to the cultural script of decline.

And here's the truth: you don't need to be a nun, a genetic anomaly, or live in a Blue Zone to begin your own *Longe-Vitality* journey. You don't even need to start with a marathon. Sometimes the most powerful transformation begins with a walk around the block, a shift in diet, or a decision to reconnect with friends. All it takes is intention, a daily choice to move, nourish, rest, and connect in ways that honour your future self. The earlier you start, the richer those extra years will be.

YOU FORGE YOUR OWN PATH THROUGH LIFE

If you come from a family where disease or early death is common, it's easy to feel like the flow of your river – it's strength and direction – has already been determined. But that resignation is outdated.

Modern science, particularly the field of epigenetics, has shown us that our genes aren't static. They're more like scripts or songs that can be edited, adapted, and even rewritten depending on how we live. Think of your genes as the keys of a grand piano. Every one of us inherits a unique set of keys, some tuned to harmonious notes, others prone to dissonance. But here's the empowering truth: the presence of a key doesn't mean it has to be played. Your daily choices, how you move, what you eat, how you manage stress, the quality of your sleep, the people you surround yourself with, are the fingers on the keys.

A family history of heart disease, diabetes, or dementia doesn't have to be a life sentence. Studies show that lifestyle changes – regular physical activity, a nutrient-rich diet, meaningful social connections, and a resilient mindset – can switch off harmful gene expression and activate protective genes.[21]

So, instead of seeing yourself as a mere listener of the song of your life, with no control over the melody or conclusion, remember – you have far more control than your DNA would have you believe. The music of your life is still being written, and you're the composer.

RUN DOC'S LONGE-VITALITY TIPS

1

Genes are not destiny.
While genetics play a role, up to 90 percent of ageing is
shaped by lifestyle and environment. The power is in your
hands.

2

Move with purpose daily.
Whether it's a walk, dancing, or gardening, movement
adds years to your life and life to your years.

3

Cultivate connection.
Call a friend. Join a group. Hug your family. Social ties are
among the most powerful predictors of longevity.

4

Live with meaning.
Purpose isn't optional, it's essential. Find something that
gets you out of bed with a smile. Then do it, again and
again.

5

Eat and sleep like you mean it.
Prioritise whole foods. Stay hydrated. Protect your sleep
like it's sacred. Because it is.

THE RIVER IS ALREADY FLOWING

You don't need a perfect family history or elite fitness to change your trajectory. You need one thing: willingness. Each decision you make, from taking the stairs, to calling a friend, to making time for purpose, is a vote for a longer, more vital life. It's time to stop seeing ageing as a burden and start seeing it as a long-distance adventure worth preparing for. It's not about how long you live – it's about how alive you feel while you're living.

CHAPTER 4

STRIDE BY STRIDE

BUILDING THE FOUNDATION OF LONGE-VITALITY THROUGH MOVEMENT

*"There is magic in movement.
Yes, movement is medicine."*

– Michael D'Aulerio

MOVEMENT – A POWERFUL PILLAR OF LONGE-VITALITY

Longe-Vitality isn't achieved through a single breakthrough or secret supplement, but rather through a series of small, sustainable decisions made day after day, stride by stride. Of all the foundational habits that support a long, vital life, movement stands above the rest. It's simple, powerful, and available to almost everyone.

Movement isn't just exercise; it's a form of expression, a discipline, a celebration of what the body can do, even as it ages. This chapter explores the importance of building a sustainable aerobic base, the bedrock of physical vitality, and how this base, when reinforced by strength, flexibility, and consistency, becomes one of the most potent tools for ageing well.

THE AEROBIC BASE: A LIFELONG ENGINE

The human body is designed for movement, and aerobic activity, whether it's walking, jogging, swimming, or cycling, aligns perfectly with its preferred rhythm. From an evolutionary standpoint, our ancestors thrived because they moved frequently and steadily, covering long distances to hunt, gather, and explore. Today, aerobic exercise continues to serve as one of the most potent drivers of health and vitality.

When you engage in aerobic activity, you strengthen your heart and lungs, enhance blood circulation, and improve the efficiency with which oxygen and nutrients are delivered throughout the body. It helps regulate blood sugar, supports healthy blood pressure, and optimises cholesterol profiles. Beyond the physical, aerobic movement triggers the release of endorphins and brain-derived neurotrophic factor (BDNF), chemicals that elevate mood, reduce anxiety, and sharpen mental clarity.

Perhaps most importantly, aerobic exercise lays the metabolic foundation for all other aspects of health. It improves mitochondrial function, increases metabolic flexibility, and builds endurance, making everyday activities easier and other forms of training more effective. Simply put, a strong aerobic base doesn't just help you live longer; it helps you live better, with more energy, resilience, and joy in the years you gain.

A pivotal 2022 meta-analysis that synthesised data from millions of participants found that just 150 minutes of moderate-intensity aerobic activity per week – the equivalent of a brisk 20-minute walk each day – is associated with a 19 to 25 percent reduction in the risk of premature death from any cause. This is a modest investment of time for a significant return in both lifespan and healthspan. The benefits were consistent across age groups, underscoring the fact that movement is a universal prescription for wellbeing.[1]

Building on these findings, a 2024 study revealed even

more compelling evidence when results were stratified by sex. Women engaging in regular aerobic exercise experienced a remarkable 24 percent reduction in all-cause mortality, while men saw a 15 percent reduction.[2] These figures highlight an important truth: while both sexes benefit substantially from regular movement, women may enjoy a particularly pronounced protective effect, possibly due to differences in cardiovascular physiology and hormonal responses to exercise.

The message is clear: our bodies respond profoundly to consistent movement. Aerobic exercise strengthens the heart, improves circulation, regulates metabolic function, and reduces inflammation, all of which contribute to lower disease risk. The earlier in life we begin, the greater the cumulative benefits over time. However, the research also offers a hopeful note: it's never too late to start. Even beginning in midlife or later can yield measurable gains in longevity and quality of life.

In the equation of healthy ageing, movement isn't optional – it's the foundation.

FAUJA SINGH: THE CENTENARIAN STRIDER

One of the most remarkable embodiments of the principle that movement matters at any age is Fauja Singh, affectionately known as the 'Turbaned Tornado'. Born in 1911 in Punjab, India, Fauja spent much of his early life as a farmer, walking miles through his fields each day. But he never considered himself an athlete. In fact, as a child, he was so frail he couldn't walk until the age of 5, and he was teased for his skinny frame. However, in later years, his life took a dramatic turn.

After immigrating to the UK in the 1990s, Fauka endured devastating personal losses: the tragic deaths of his wife and son. Struggling with grief and loneliness, he turned to jogging to process his pain. Step by step, Fauja found not only a way to cope with sorrow but also a renewed sense of purpose and identity.

At the age of 89, he completed his first marathon, an accomplishment most people half his age never achieve.[3] His training was simple: he avoided processed foods, ate a light vegetarian diet, walked or ran daily, and maintained a calm, stress-free outlook on life.[4] The results were extraordinary. In 2004, at 93, Fauja completed the London Marathon in 6 hours and 7 minutes – a personal best for the race. In 2011, at the age of 100, he became the oldest person ever to finish a full marathon, completing the Toronto Waterfront Marathon in 8 hours and 11 minutes.[5] Even after officially retiring from competitive racing at 101, he continued to run shorter distances and participate in charity events, inspiring countless others.[6]

What makes Fauja's story so powerful isn't just his achievements, but the way they dismantle common assumptions about ageing. He didn't begin running as a young man. He didn't rely on cutting-edge sports science, expensive gear, or elite coaching. Instead, his success was built on consistency, simplicity, and a deep belief in the value of movement. His life is living proof that the human body, when cared for and used as nature intended, is capable of remarkable endurance, well beyond the age society labels 'old'.

Fauja Singh's legacy is more than his records; it's his example. He reminds us that it's never too late to start, movement can be a source of healing, and purpose can be rediscovered at any age. For runners, walkers, and anyone seeking a healthier, more vibrant life, Fauja's journey offers an unshakable truth: your age isn't your limit – your mindset is.

DIANA NYAD:
THE LONG SWIM TO DESTINY

If Fauja Singh shows us the power of persistent steps, Diana Nyad teaches us the value of enduring waves. In September 2013, at the age of 64, Diana became the first person to swim from Cuba to Florida without a shark cage, a 110-mile (177-kilometre) crossing that took nearly 53 hours of continuous, unassisted swimming through open ocean.[7] The feat was physically extraordinary, but the backstory is what makes it legendary.

Diana had first attempted the swim in her late 20s, but strong currents, box jellyfish stings, and unpredictable weather stopped her. Decades later, in her 60s, she returned to the challenge, not as the same athlete she once was, but as a more seasoned, resilient, and strategically trained version of herself. Between 2011 and 2013, she made four unsuccessful attempts before finally succeeding on her fifth try.[8] Each 'failure' became a lesson in patience, adaptation, and perseverance.

Her preparation in later life wasn't solely about high-volume swim training. It included strength work, mental conditioning, and gradual aerobic development built over years.[9] Diana's regimen wasn't athletic punishment, but an act of devotion, a daily investment in a dream that demanded both physical and psychological readiness.

"You're never too old to chase your dreams," she said after reaching the Florida shore.[10] That statement wasn't mere motivation; it was lived experience. At an age when many consider scaling back ambitions, Diana was increasing hers, proving that human potential is far less limited by years than by mindset and preparation.

Her story underlines that an aerobic base is more than just

a foundation for cardiovascular endurance; it's a platform for resilience, grit, and mental stamina. This same base helps marathon runners push through the infamous 'wall' at around kilometre 30 and enables active centenarians to climb stairs, travel independently, or carry their grandchildren. Aerobic capacity supports the body's oxygen delivery systems, regulates metabolic health, and fortifies the mind against fatigue.[11] In Diana's case, it also provided the physiological bedrock needed to swim steadily for more than 2 full days without pause.

Her triumph wasn't simply about athletic prowess, but about redefining limits. It demonstrated that ageing doesn't have to mean decline, and with consistent, intentional training, the later decades of life can be a stage for some of our boldest performances. Diana's long swim was more than a crossing of ocean waters; it was a crossing of perceived boundaries, reminding us that determination, strategic preparation, and a strong aerobic engine can carry us further than we imagine.

INTERMITTENT WALKING THERAPY: ACCESSIBLE AEROBIC POWER

As the Run Doc, I've worked with countless people who feel daunted by the idea of exercise, especially older adults or those new to movement. It's common to hear, "I can't run" or, "I'm too out of shape for the gym." But here's the truth: you don't have to run a marathon or lift heavy weights to boost your health. Aerobic fitness, the engine that powers longevity, can be built with simple, manageable movement. That's where intermittent walking therapy (IWT) comes in.

IWT is an approach designed to fit seamlessly into everyday life. One study demonstrated that high-intensity IWT – alternating between brisk walking and a slower recovery pace – improves joint function, aerobic capacity, and blood pressure in older adults.[12] Unlike continuous walking at a steady pace, this interval style activates the aerobic system more effectively by gently pushing your heart rate up, then allowing recovery, without undue joint stress or overwhelming fatigue.

The IWT Routine: Simple, Effective, Scalable

Here's a basic IWT routine that anyone can try, no special gear or gym membership required:

- Walk briskly for 3 minutes

- Slow down to an easy, comfortable pace for 3 minutes

- Repeat this cycle five times for a total of 30 minutes

It's that simple. The brisk segments push your cardiovascular system; the slower segments allow your body to recover and prepare for the next interval of effort. This cycling of intensity mimics interval training principles but without the high-impact strain of running or vigorous gym workouts.

Why IWT Works So Well

From a physiological standpoint, IWT improves aerobic power by encouraging the body to adapt to varying demands on the cardiovascular and muscular systems. According to research, interval-based activities promote greater improvements in cardiorespiratory fitness and other important biomarkers than continuous moderate exercise alone.[13] Essentially, your heart and lungs become more efficient; your muscles get stronger and more resilient, and your energy metabolism improves. In older adults, these changes translate into better walking speed, reduced fall risk, and enhanced independence.

IWT Is Joint-Friendly and Mentally Manageable

Many older adults struggle with arthritis or joint pain that makes continuous moderate to vigorous exercise uncomfortable or unsustainable. Because IWT alternates intensity, it reduces the risk of overuse injuries while still delivering aerobic benefits. The breaks in pace are also mentally refreshing, making the routine less daunting and easier to stick with.

Another plus? IWT sessions can be done anywhere, indoors

or outdoors, rain or shine. A hallway, a park trail, or even a shopping mall provides plenty of space. This accessibility removes barriers that often prevent people from starting or maintaining exercise habits.

The Power of Consistency

If there's one lesson I emphasise as the Run Doc, it's this: consistency beats intensity. You don't need to be a gym warrior or a marathoner to reap huge health rewards. Regular, manageable movement like IWT gradually improves your aerobic base – the foundation for cardiovascular health, metabolism, brain function, and emotional resilience.

Imagine this. Just 30 minutes per day, 5 days per week, of intermittent walking promotes healthy ageing and reduces the risk of many age-related diseases, including cardiovascular disease, hypertension, type 2 diabetes, and cancer.[14] Even better, the benefits multiply when you maintain this habit long term.

The Art of Getting Started

If you're new to exercise or returning after a break, start with what feels achievable. Maybe begin with just two cycles (12 minutes) and build up over weeks. Wear comfortable shoes, stay hydrated, and listen to your body. If you feel dizzy or short of breath, slow down and take longer recovery breaks.

Most importantly, celebrate progress. Every step is a win towards better health. IWT isn't a punishment; it's a pathway to empowerment, showing you that aerobic fitness is within reach, no matter your age or starting point.

STRENGTH TRAINING: SUPPORTING THE STRIDE

I can't stress enough how vital strength training is for runners and active people of all ages. While aerobic exercise is king when it comes to cardiovascular health and endurance, resistance training is the often-overlooked queen that keeps your body strong, balanced, and resilient. If running is the engine, strength training is the frame that holds everything together.

Here's the thing: as we age, we naturally lose muscle mass and strength in a process called sarcopenia. Starting in our 30s, muscle tissue declines gradually, accelerating after age 60. This loss isn't just about looking toned; it's a major risk factor for falls, fractures, loss of independence, and slower recovery from injuries. For runners, weak muscles mean compromised stride mechanics, poor posture, and increased injury risk. The good news? Sarcopenia isn't inevitable. Just twice-weekly resistance training sessions can reverse this trend and rebuild strength.[15]

Research demonstrates that resistance training is a power-house for health beyond just building muscles and can create significant improvements in:

- **Blood pressure:** Strength training helps regulate vascular function, reducing hypertension risk.[16]

- **Glycaemic control:** Muscle contractions improve insulin sensitivity, which is crucial for preventing or managing type 2 diabetes.[17]

- **Lipid profiles:** Regular resistance exercise can lower LDL ('bad' cholesterol) and raise HDL ('good' cholesterol).[18]

- **Body composition:** Building muscle boosts resting metabolic rate, helping maintain a healthy weight and reduce fat mass.[19]

But the benefits don't stop there. When you combine strength training with aerobic exercise, the synergy is powerful. This combination reduces the risk of falls and fractures by improving balance, coordination, and bone density.[20] It also protects against metabolic syndrome and cognitive decline by keeping your brain and body connected and responsive.[21]

Remember, strength training isn't about bulking up unless that's your goal. For most of us, it's about preserving function, maintaining the muscle power needed to climb stairs, carry groceries, play with grandkids, and keep running smoothly and pain-free.

Simple, Effective Strength Training Moves You Can Do Anywhere

If you're new to resistance work or short on time, start small. You don't need fancy gyms or heavy weights. Your own body and resistance bands can do wonders. Here are my go-to foundational moves for runners:

- **Bodyweight squats:** This classic move strengthens your legs and hips, which are vital for a strong, stable stride. Stand with feet shoulder width apart, lower your hips back and down as if sitting in a chair, then rise back up. Aim for 2 to 3 sets of 10 to 15 reps.

- **Resistance band rows:** Strengthening the upper back improves posture and running form, reducing risk of shoulder and neck tension. Anchor a resistance band at waist height, pull the handles toward your torso, squeezing your shoulder blades together. Two to three sets of 12 to 15 reps work well.

- **Wall or counter push-ups:** A gentle way to build upper body strength without overloading the shoulders. Stand facing a wall or kitchen counter, place your hands shoulder width apart, lower your chest towards the surface, then push back. Start with 2 sets of 10 reps and increase as you get stronger.

TIPS FOR STRENGTH TRAINING SUCCESS AND SAFETY

- Focus on controlled movements, don't rush. Quality beats quantity every time.
- Aim to progress gradually by increasing reps, sets, or resistance as you adapt.
- Listen to your body and allow recovery time between sessions.
- If you're unsure about technique, seek guidance from a qualified trainer or physical therapist.

As the Run Doc, I want you to think of strength training as insurance, not just for your running, but for your life. The stronger your muscles, the better you can withstand the wear and tear of daily living and keep doing what you love with joy and independence.

So, lace up your shoes for that run, but don't skip those strength sessions. They're the secret weapon that will keep your stride strong and your body resilient for decades to come.

ANCIENT WISDOM MEETS MODERN SCIENCE

Modern science has increasingly confirmed what our elders have intuitively understood for centuries: the key to healthy ageing lies in consistent movement. The phrase "move it or lose it" captures this essential truth. Physical activity isn't just about maintaining muscle tone or cardiovascular fitness; it's a holistic approach that supports the entire body and mind through the ageing process.

The holistic benefits of movement, from strengthening bones and muscles to nurturing brain plasticity, makes it the single most comprehensive and accessible tool we have for extending our healthspan, not just our lifespan. Movement is medicine, but it's also a ritual, a social connector, and a source of joy. It empowers us to remain independent, engaged, and vital well into our later years.

The lives of active elders worldwide, from Fauja Singh to

everyday people walking, gardening, or dancing, reflect these scientific principles. Their longevity and quality of life are proof that consistent, balanced movement nurtures both body and mind across decades.

Incorporating movement daily is a proactive investment in health, enabling us to age with grace and purpose. The science is clear, the evidence overwhelming, and the prescription simple: move often and move smartly.

RUN DOC'S LONGE-VITALITY TIPS

1

Start slow, stay consistent.
Don't chase heroics. Begin with 10 to 15 minutes of walking each day, and build gradually. The secret isn't speed; it's sustainability. Consistency creates change.

2

Practise intermittent walking therapy.
Alternate your pace – a minute brisk, a minute easy – to stimulate your cardiovascular system without strain. Perfect for beginners, beneficial for elites. Gentle rhythm, powerful results.

3

Add simple strength training.
Twice per week, include body-weight squats, resistance-band work, or gentle yoga.
Even light resistance builds muscle integrity and protects against age-related decline.

RUN DOC'S LONGE-VITALITY TIPS

4

Keep moving throughout the day.
Health isn't made in one workout; it's woven through your day. Walk after meals. Take the stairs. Garden. Stretch. Dance around the kitchen. Every 'movement snack' adds to your vitality bank.

5

Listen to your body.
Pain is a message. Fatigue is a guide. Learn the art of discernment – between effort and harm, between drive and rest. True longevity honours recovery as much as movement.

6

Use movement as mindfulness.
Let walking or running become meditation in motion. One foot. One breath. One moment. Move not just to live longer, but to live better.

EVERY STEP IS A SEED OF LONGE-VITALITY

The great lie of ageing is that decline is inevitable. But the truth, revealed in the lives of Fauja Singh, Diana Nyad, and countless others, is that we can grow stronger, more vital, and more resilient through simple, intentional movement.

Building an aerobic base isn't about chasing records. It's about cultivating a sustainable rhythm of health, a foundation that supports everything else: cognition, strength, spirit, and independence.

Stride by stride, we move towards *Longe-Vitality*.

Stride by stride, we reclaim what ageing tries to take.

Stride by stride, we write a new story – of movement, magic, and momentum that lasts a lifetime.

CHAPTER 5

THE HEARTBEAT OF HEALTH

CARDIO AND CELLULAR VITALITY

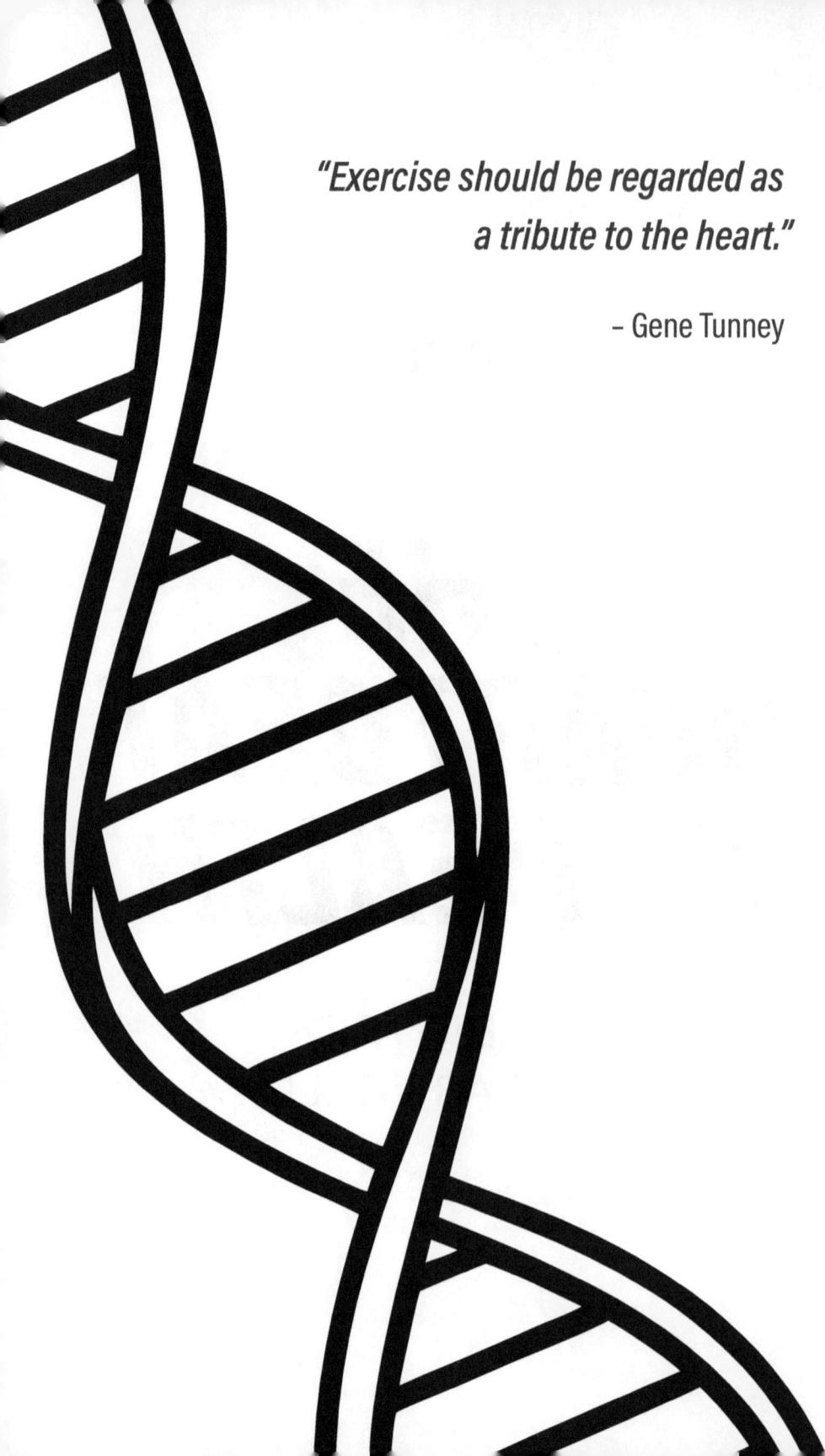

"Exercise should be regarded as a tribute to the heart."

– Gene Tunney

LET YOUR HEARTBEAT BE YOUR COMPASS

The steady rhythm of the human heart is more than a biological beat; it's the tempo of our vitality. In the journey of *Longe-Vitality*, this heartbeat becomes a compass pointing us towards long life, robust energy, and cellular resilience. Cardiovascular health is the foundation of physical endurance and a key driver of mitochondrial function, immune response, emotional regulation, and even brain health.

If movement is medicine, then the heart is both doctor and patient. It responds directly to the choices we make – how we move, how we breathe, how we eat, how we rest. The good news? We can influence it. In a world obsessed with genetic testing and longevity hacks, the evidence continues to affirm one elegant truth: endurance matters.

THE ENDURANCE-LONGEVITY CONNECTION

Decades of data have drawn a clear line between cardiovascular fitness and extended healthspan. Endurance exercise, whether it's running, brisk walking, hiking, or cycling, not only strengthens the heart muscle but also lowers resting heart rate, improves blood pressure, boosts HDL cholesterol, and reduces inflammation. These markers aren't just good for the heart; they sustain nearly every system in the body.

Research confirms that both aerobic and resistance exercises contribute substantially to longevity and heart health, with aerobic activity, such as running or fast walking, having the most direct impact on cardiovascular endurance.[1] These effects aren't theoretical. They show up in blood panels, heart scans, energy levels, and, ultimately, in the number of years we remain vital and independent.

MITOCHONDRIA: THE CELL'S ENDURANCE ENGINE

The benefits of endurance exercise extend to our smallest building blocks: the mitochondria, tiny energy factories inside our cells. Mitochondria take in oxygen and nutrients to produce ATP, the energy currency of life. But with age and inactivity, these powerhouses falter. Mitochondrial dysfunction contributes to fatigue, muscle loss, cognitive decline, and a host of age-related diseases.

Fortunately, endurance exercise acts like a cellular reset. A pivotal 2023 study found that lifelong endurance athletes have more efficient and better-connected mitochondrial networks than untrained individuals. Their muscle cells showed superior energy output and better oxygen utilisation compared to sedentary peers of the same age.[2]

Additional research further underscores the critical role of physical activity in boosting cellular health: regular endurance training significantly improves mitochondrial function, biogenesis (new mitochondria formation), and cellular repair mechanisms.[3] Translation? The more we move with purpose, the younger our cells behave.

HEART RATE VARIABILITY – LISTENING TO THE HEART'S WHISPER

One of the most sensitive indicators of cardiovascular and autonomic health is heart rate variability (HRV): the variation in time between consecutive heartbeats. Unlike heart rate, which simply counts beats per minute, HRV reveals how adaptable the body is to stress, recovery, and change. A higher HRV is generally linked to better cardiovascular fitness, emotional resilience, and even immune function.

Endurance athletes tend to have high HRV – a sign of a nervous system that's in tune and flexible. Importantly, HRV can be improved with consistent training, sleep hygiene, breathwork, and mindfulness. With the rise of wearable tech, anyone can monitor their HRV trends and use the data as a feedback loop to balance intensity, recovery, and rest.

REAL-LIFE INSPIRATIONS: WALKING WITH GIANTS

Now let's meet a couple more real-life inspirations who dared to defy the narrative around ageing and took their healthspans into their own hands.

1. Ernestine Shepherd – USA

At 89, Ernestine Shepherd defies every stereotype about ageing. Although now a bodybuilder, marathoner, and daily walker, she didn't begin serious training until her 50s. Today, she continues to wake before dawn, meditates, runs or walks daily, and eats a disciplined, nutrient-rich diet.

Her message is clear: "Age is nothing but a number."[4] Ernestine embodies the cellular vitality that comes from consistent cardiovascular training. Beyond her physical strength lies a deeper truth: movement keeps her mentally sharp, emotionally grounded, and spiritually energised.

2. Carlos Soria – Spain

High in the Himalayas, Carlos Soria continues to chase peaks, literally. This Spanish mountaineer didn't attempt his first 8,000-metre summit until age 51. Since then, he's summited 12 of the world's 14 highest peaks, most after turning 60.[5] At age 84, he was still attempting Dhaulagiri, one of two of the

14 he's yet to conquer.[6] How does he do it? His secret isn't superhuman strength, but aerobic capacity. He maintains an impeccable endurance base through daily hiking, cycling, and structured training.[7]

Carlos shows that even at extreme altitudes and advanced age, the human engine, when well-maintained, can perform astonishing feats.

CARDIOVASCULAR ENDURANCE AS PREVENTIVE MEDICINE

The benefits of cardiovascular endurance extend well beyond the heart, touching nearly every system in the body.

Cognitive Function

Regular aerobic exercise has been shown to increase hippocampal volume, the region of the brain central to memory formation, and improve executive function. A landmark 2010 randomised controlled trial found that walking 40 minutes per week not only enlarges the hippocampus in older adults but also improves spatial memory.[8] Meta-analyses confirm that sustained cardiovascular activity is associated with a lower risk of dementia and cognitive decline.[9]

Mood Regulation

Aerobic movement stimulates the release of serotonin, dopamine, and endorphins, neurochemicals linked to positive mood, motivation, and resilience. Research indicates that regular aerobic exercise can be as effective as pharmacological interventions for mild to moderate depression, while also reducing anxiety symptoms.[10]

Immunity and Inflammation

Cardiovascular fitness is linked to lower levels of chronic low-grade inflammation. Research demonstrates that moderate to vigorous aerobic activity enhances immune surveillance, potentially reducing susceptibility to infections and improving vaccine response in older adults.[11] This anti-inflammatory effect also contributes to the prevention of many age-related diseases.

Metabolic Health

Endurance training improves insulin sensitivity and glucose regulation, significantly lowering the risk of developing type 2 diabetes. Research has shown that individuals engaging in regular aerobic exercise achieve better glycaemic control and body composition improvements, even without dietary changes.[12]

What Does It All Mean?

Taken together, these findings reinforce a powerful truth: cardiovascular endurance isn't just about a stronger heart; it's about creating a more resilient body and mind. By integrating regular aerobic movement into daily life, whether through running, brisk walking, cycling, or swimming, we invest in sharper thinking, steadier moods, stronger immunity, and metabolic stability. In essence, a strong heart supports a strong body, which in turn sustains a vibrant, independent life well into later decades.

TAKE CONTROL OF YOUR CARDIOVASCULAR HEALTH

Dr Daniel Levy, the longtime director of the Framingham Heart Study, distilled decades of epidemiological research into one life-affirming insight: "We can control our destiny even if we can't control the genes that we inherit." This isn't mere optimism; it's the scientific reality borne out by generations of longitudinal data.

I've said it before, and I'll say it again – while our genetic code may load the gun, our daily habits often pull or, more importantly, keep the finger off the trigger. We may be born with an increased risk of cardiovascular disease, diabetes, or neurodegenerative disorders, but research consistently shows that lifestyle choices, particularly regular movement, can mitigate or even override much of that inherited risk.[13] In this light, exercise becomes less about chasing performance metrics and more about tipping the odds in our favour.

Endurance activity, whether brisk walking, running, cycling, or swimming, is a particularly powerful lever. Studies have demonstrated that consistent aerobic exercise improves vascular elasticity, reduces systemic inflammation, and promotes metabolic efficiency.[14] These effects don't just protect the heart; they also safeguard the brain, bones, immune system, and emotional wellbeing. It's the biological equivalent of a diversified investment portfolio, protecting multiple systems with one habit.

Importantly, the benefits compound over time. Just as small, daily deposits grow into significant wealth, short bouts of movement, done persistently over decades, translate into extra years of independence and vitality (*Longe-Vitality*). This reframes ageing from an inevitable decline into a dynamic process we can influence. In my experience, this control is deeply empowering. Patients who once felt at the mercy of their family history often discover a renewed sense of agency once they experience the tangible effects of training: a steadier pulse, easier breathing, better sleep, and sharper focus. These aren't abstract promises; they're lived, measurable outcomes.

While no one can guarantee immortality, we can, as Dr Levy suggests, dramatically alter the trajectory of our health.

The path is neither glamorous nor extreme; it's grounded in consistent, intentional movement. Each workout is a quiet act of defiance against genetic fatalism and a deliberate investment in a longer, more vibrant life.

RUN DOC'S LONGE-VITALITY TIPS

1

Move daily, endure weekly.
Aim for at least 150 to 300 minutes of moderate-intensity movement each week – brisk walking, running, hiking, or swimming. Variety builds sustainability. Consistency builds longevity. Motion is the body's natural medicine.

2

Monitor HRV (heart rate variability), not just BPM (beats per minute).
Your HRV is a mirror of resilience and recovery. Use wearables wisely – don't chase numbers, observe trends.

3

Train your mitochondria.
These tiny powerhouses are the spark of longevity. Stimulate them through:
» Endurance exercise (the best biogenesis booster)
» Fasted walks for metabolic flexibility
» Intervals to ignite cellular renewal
» Build your base, then build your fire.

RUN DOC'S LONGE-VITALITY TIPS

4

Inspire yourself with elders in motion.
Let legends like Ernestine Shepherd and Carlos Soria remind you that age isn't the enemy; inertia is. Better yet, seek out the everyday heroes around you – the local runners, walkers, and gardeners who move with purpose and grace.

5

Prioritise recovery.
Endurance is forged in training and built in recovery. Sleep 7 to 9 hours per night. Move gently on rest days. Fuel your body with antioxidant-rich whole foods, omega-3s, and colour on your plate. Rest isn't weakness; it's where resilience grows.

6

Walk with purpose.
Never underestimate the humble walk. It's the daily rhythm of Blue Zone longevity cultures and the quiet habit shared by my two grandmothers – a ritual that kept their minds sharp and spirits grounded. Every step is a vote for vitality. Walk often. Walk mindfully. Walk for life.

THE FINAL BEAT

Whether you're climbing Everest like Carlos, building muscle like Ernestine, or simply walking to the local shop like FC and SL Wong, one thing is clear: the heartbeat, both literal and metaphorical, remains at the core of long, vital living.

In every stride, every breath, every beat, we improve not just our bodies, but our futures. The key to Longe-Vitality isn't locked in our DNA. It pulses inside us, waiting to be strengthened, day by day, mile by mile.

Keep your heart moving. Keep your life expanding.

CHAPTER 6

THE STRENGTH TO ENDURE

MUSCLES, BONES, AND MINDSET

"A hero is an ordinary individual who finds the strength to persevere and endure in spite of overwhelming obstacles."

– Christopher Reeve, Superman

THE QUIET MIGHT OF EVERYDAY HEROES

We often misunderstand strength. We imagine it in the realm of athletes or warriors, people with bulging biceps, racks of medals, or the kind of physiques that dominate Instagram feeds. But the truest strength, the kind that fuels *Longe-Vitality*, is often quiet, humble, and invisible to the casual observer.

It looks like my grandmother kneeling to tend her plants every morning before sunrise, hands buried in the earth, back curved like she was in prayer. It looks like my other grandmother squatting to stir a wok over a low stove well into her 80s, steam fogging her glasses as she cooked for her family. Neither woman owned a pair of dumbbells. They had never set foot in a gym or followed a formal exercise program. But they had resilience. They had routine. They had purpose.

Though they never spoke of musculoskeletal strength, they embodied it daily. Science now calls this 'functional strength', the ability to perform everyday movements like lifting, squatting, bending, and balancing with efficiency and safety. For my grandmothers, it was simply life. Their movements – carrying groceries, drawing water, washing clothes, climbing stairs – weren't structured workouts but natural extensions of living in a way that demanded regular use of every muscle group.

Modern research affirms what my grandmothers' lives demonstrated intuitively: strength is one of the most important predictors of healthy ageing. Studies show that grip strength, a simple marker of overall muscle function, strongly predicts longevity, independence, and reduced risk of chronic disease.[1] Additionally, resistance and weight-bearing movements, whether performed in a gym or as part of daily chores, maintain bone density, protect against sarcopenia (age-related muscle loss), and help regulate metabolic health.[2]

Perhaps most importantly, my grandmothers' strength was purposeful. They didn't lift for aesthetics. They moved to care for a garden, to prepare meals, to serve others. Purpose (or *ikigai*) infused their physicality. They didn't run ultramarathons or chase world records. But they moved, daily, deliberately, and without fanfare. They aged with strength, autonomy, and dignity. And in doing so, they quietly modelled a truth that the fittest of athletes sometimes forget: the ultimate goal of physical capacity isn't to post a faster time or lift a heavier weight, but to live fully, independently, and joyfully for as long as possible.

The quiet might of these everyday heroes reminds us that the foundation of *Longe-Vitality* isn't built in gyms alone, but in kitchens, gardens, markets, and the small, repeated actions that comprise a life.

GOLDEN BOLT: HIDEKICHI MIYAZAKI, JAPAN'S SPRINTING CENTENARIAN

Japan's Hidekichi Miyazaki, fondly nicknamed the 'Golden Bolt', redefined what the later chapters of life could look like. Remarkably, he didn't take up competitive sprinting until his 90s. Yet at age 105, he lined up for the 100 metres at the Kyoto Masters Games and crossed the finish line in 42.22 seconds. Then, with a gleam in his eye, he struck Usain Bolt's signature lightning pose. The photograph went viral. The message, captured in that moment, was immortal: old age isn't an expiry date for vitality.[3]

Hidekichi's achievements weren't born of luck or fleeting inspiration. They were the result of intentional consistent practice, sprinting and throwing shot-put daily – except when it was raining.[4] His story illustrates a critical nuance often missed in fitness culture: mobility without strength is fragile; strength without purpose is hollow.

The Golden Bolt, an exemplar of strength and a hero to many, reminds us that human potential is elastic, even deep into the winter years. We can't turn back the biological clock, but we can wind it forward with more resilience, capacity, and joy than many imagine possible. His legacy is a call to action: don't wait for the 'right time' to begin moving – start now, start small, and keep going. It's never too late, or too early, to step up and become the hero.

BONES ARE LIVING STRUCTURES – AND THEY THRIVE ON LOAD

Where muscle goes, bone follows. Our skeleton isn't a fixed frame; it's a living, breathing structure that listens to how we move and adapts accordingly. Every time we walk, climb, squat, or carry something heavy, tiny sensors in our bones send signals to cells that either build or break down tissue. It's a constant conversation between our daily actions and our long-term skeletal health. This is the essence of Wolff's law: bones remodel themselves based on the forces they experience. Load them regularly, and they'll grow denser, stronger, and more resilient. Neglect them, and, like a bridge left to rust, they slowly weaken.[5]

A 2025 meta-analysis found that progressive exercise training – which can include a range of activities such as resistance training, aerobic exercise, and even tai chi – increases bone mineral density and is a promising intervention for people suffering from, or at risk of developing, osteoporosis.[6]

For women, especially postmenopause, intervention becomes urgent. The decline in oestrogen, once a powerful guardian of bone health, can accelerate loss of bone density, tipping the scales towards osteopenia or osteoporosis. Fortunately, targeted resistance training and impact exercises, such as running and jumping, can slow or even reverse this decline.[7] The message is clear: load your bones or lose them.

But bone health is about more than mineral density. It's

about balance, posture, and coordination, factors that dramatically reduce the risk of falls. In the world of *Longe-Vitality*, prevention is as powerful as cure. Strength training for the legs and core, combined with balance drills, doesn't just make bones denser; it makes the whole body safer.

Consider Sister Madonna Buder, our 'Iron Nun', who was still competing in triathlons in her 90s. Her frame, though slender, was built from decades of consistent training: running, cycling, swimming, lifting. Her bones weren't brittle. They were endurance-built, living proof that skeletal strength isn't a gift of youth, but a reward for consistent movement.

When we think about *Longe-Vitality*, we often focus on the heart, lungs, and mind, but our skeleton is just as critical. Without strong bones, the journey is cut short. Every hike, every squat, every step with a grocery bag in hand is more than movement; it's a message to your body: *I still need you strong.*

Your bones aren't asking for perfection. They're asking for consistency. Challenge them regularly, and they'll respond in kind. That's the promise of living structures: given a reason, they'll adapt, and in that adaptation lies the foundation for a long, vital life.

THE STRENGTH OF EVERYDAY MOVEMENT: LESSONS FROM THE GENERATIONAL 100 STUDY

In the snow-covered hills of Norway, researchers found something remarkable: not just longevity, but vitality in motion. The Generational 100 Study, one of the most comprehensive long-term investigations into exercise and ageing, followed hundreds of older adults over more than a decade to uncover how physical activity shapes the arc of ageing.

The results are clear and compelling. Those who maintain regular, moderate to vigorous exercise – such as brisk walking, cycling, or cross-country skiing – not only live longer but also preserve cardiorespiratory fitness, balance, and independence well into their 80s. More importantly, the benefits extend beyond lifespan to healthspan: fewer hospitalisations, greater mobility, sharper cognition, and higher quality of life.[8]

The study reinforces a timeless truth: movement is medicine, but it doesn't need to come from a gym. Functional activity – climbing stairs, carrying groceries, rising from low chairs, or working in the garden – builds the strength, balance, and confidence required for real life. These simple, purposeful actions mirror what exercise scientists call the SAID principle: specific adaptation to imposed demands. In other words, the body best adapts to the movements it regularly performs.

In this light, longevity isn't an accident of good genetics or mild climates. It's a practiced skill – the art of staying strong enough to keep living life on your own terms. Whether that means hiking a local hill, tending to a garden, or simply walking without fear of falling, the message is universal: everyday movement matters.

SNOW-STRONG MOVES YOU CAN USE ANYWHERE

Inspired by the 'Generational 100' philosophy from snow-covered Norway.

The following three drills don't require a gym, just your body, a little space, and a willingness to move with purpose. Aim for 2 to 3 rounds, 2 to 3 times per week.

1. Icy Curb Step-Overs
- Why: Builds hip mobility and balance, leading to fall prevention.
- How: Place a small box, foam block, or sturdy stack of books in front of you. Step over slowly without touching the

'curb', lifting your knees high. Step back the same way.
- Run Doc tip: Add a light ankle weight for an extra challenge. Your hips will thank you next winter.

2. Low Chair Stand-Ups
- Why: Strengthens quads, glutes, and core for rising from seats with ease.
- How: Sit on a low stool or chair (knee angle greater than 90 degrees). Cross arms over chest, lean forward slightly, and stand without using your hands. Slowly lower yourself back down.
- Run Doc tip: Try this on one leg for advanced balance and strength.

3. Firewood Carries
- Why: Boosts grip, posture, and 'real-world' carrying power.
- How: Hold a pair of heavy objects (buckets, water jugs, shopping bags) at your sides. Walk 20 to 30 metres with a tall posture and steady core.

- Run Doc tip: Imagine you're carrying logs to a cabin. It's more fun when you give the work a story.

MUSCLE: THE UNSUNG METABOLIC HERO ORGAN

We often think of muscle as simply mechanical, a system of pulleys and levers designed to move us through space. But muscle is metabolic gold. Far from being inert, skeletal muscle is a living, breathing biochemical powerhouse that influences nearly every aspect of our healthspan.

Skeletal muscle is the body's largest site for insulin-mediated glucose uptake. This means it acts as a massive sponge for blood sugar, preventing excess glucose from lingering in the bloodstream where it can wreak havoc on vessels and organs. More muscle means greater capacity to store glycogen, respond to insulin, and regulate blood sugar. In this way, muscle functions as a critical defence system against type 2 diabetes, metabolic syndrome, and systemic inflammation.[9]

Modern research underscores just how profound this relationship is with studies showing that older adults with higher muscle mass have significantly better metabolic markers:

lower fasting glucose, improved cholesterol profiles, and reduced levels of inflammatory cytokines.[10] This isn't about chasing sixpacks or hypertrophy; it's about building metabolic resilience. Those with more muscle tissue aren't just stronger; they're biologically younger, their systems running smoother, with less oxidative wear and tear.

Muscle also has a remarkable role in protecting organs. It shields the heart by improving lipid metabolism and vascular function. It preserves brain health through myokines – hormone-like proteins released during muscle contraction that cross the blood-brain barrier to stimulate neurogenesis and reduce neuroinflammation.[11] It lightens the workload on the liver by improving insulin sensitivity, reducing fat deposition, and modulating inflammatory pathways. It even supports the pancreas by lowering the insulin demands of everyday living.

My grandmothers didn't know the term 'myokine'. They didn't track macros, log reps, or weigh out protein powder. But they moved. Daily. Purposefully. One worked in the paddy fields, bending and lifting under the tropical sun. The other carried baskets from the wet market, washed laundry by hand, and walked everywhere. Their labour wasn't 'exercise' in the modern sense; it was woven into life itself, and it preserved not just their legs, but also their lungs, liver, brain, and heart.

When it comes to *Longe-Vitality*, there's a recurring

theme: longevity isn't merely about avoiding disease; it's about building a physiological reserve, a buffer against the inevitable stresses of time. Muscle is that reserve. It's the armour that blunts the blows of ageing, the savings account that pays dividends when your body is under stress.

The lesson is clear: maintain your muscle, and it will maintain you. Not through brute force or vanity-driven workouts, but through consistent, functional movement that engages the largest engine in your body. Because muscle isn't just about moving you – it's about keeping every part of you alive and thriving.

STRONG BODY, STRONG MIND

"Strong body, strong mind" isn't a metaphor. It's measurable. And it's one of the most underappreciated longevity tools we have. For decades, aerobic exercise held the spotlight in discussions about healthy ageing. Yet, an emerging wave of research shows that strength training, often seen as the domain of bodybuilders, may be just as essential for a long, vibrant life.

A 2023 study concluded that resistance training significantly improves overall cognitive function and reduces symptoms of depression.[12] Therefore, when we train for strength, we're not just training our muscles, we're also training our minds, improving the very mental capacities that allow us to navigate complex tasks, adapt to change, and maintain independence in later years.

In the *Longe-Vitality* journey, strength training isn't optional; it's foundational. It shapes a body that can move freely, a mind that can think clearly, and a spirit that can face challenges with poise. The barbell, resistance band, or pull-up bar becomes more than equipment; it becomes a tool for self-renewal.

So the next time you squat, push, pull, or lunge, remember – you're not just moving iron. You're rewiring your brain, buffering yourself against depression, building resilience, and, in a very real sense, forging inner peace. A strong body is a strong mind, and both are pillars of a long, vital life.

YOU DON'T NEED A GYM, YOU NEED GRIT

For me, strength isn't defined by the weight on a barbell. It's defined by the willingness to keep showing up, whether you're lacing up running shoes, hefting laundry baskets, or doing body-weight squats beside your kitchen counter.

Grit, more than gear, predicts long-term adherence to an active lifestyle.[13] You don't need the latest biohack to build longevity. You need consistency, choosing movement daily, no matter how little. You need creativity, finding ways to turn chores into training and everyday spaces into arenas of vitality. And you need commitment, not to perfection, but to persistence.

In the end, strength isn't about lifting the heaviest dumbbell. It's about lifting yourself, again and again, when life presses down.

My grandmothers' legacies remind me: the world may change, but the essentials for a long, vital life remain remarkably simple. And then there's Hidekichi Miyazaki, our Japanese 'Golden Bolt', who chose to start sprinting in his 90s – a true inspiration. Ultimately, enduring strength isn't the result of a single act of heroism, but a lifelong rhythm of continuously showing up when it matters most.

RUN DOC'S LONGE-VITALITY TIPS

1 **Strength is for everyone, at every age.**
Whether you're 35 or 95, it's never too late to start.
Resistance training builds not just muscle, but balance,
confidence, and independence. Every rep today is an
investment in tomorrow's freedom.

2 **Load your bones, not just your muscles.**
Strong bones love a little stress. Try stair climbing, hiking,
squats, or gentle impact drills.
If impact isn't for you, resistance bands, water weights, or
mindful Pilates will keep your skeleton smiling.

3 **Function > physique.**
Forget the mirror – train for life. Practise getting up from
the floor, carrying groceries, and balancing on one foot.
These are the true tests of lifelong vitality.

4 **Muscles fuel body and mind.**
Strong muscles don't just move you; they stabilise
blood sugar, lift your mood, sharpen memory, and tame
inflammation. Muscle is medicine.

5 **Make movement sacred.**
Like Sister Madonna Buder, move as an act of devotion –
not punishment, not obligation, but a daily ritual of
gratitude for the life within.

YOU'RE STRONGER THAN YOU THINK

You don't need to be an Olympian to age like one. Every farmer who lifts hay, every elder who climbs stairs with groceries, every mother who squats to tie a child's shoelaces – these are the unsung athletes of longevity.

Strength is in your stride. Strength is in your story. Strength is in your stillness.

As Helen Keller once said, "Although the world is full of suffering, it is also full of the overcoming of it." And perhaps, just perhaps, the one who overcomes … is you. So keep lifting. Keep moving. Keep rising. One rep. One walk. One resilient day at a time.

CHAPTER 7

NUTRITION FOR LONGE-VITALITY

FUELLING THE LONG RUN

"Key to longevity ... drinking embalming fluid every year."

– Angus Young

EATING FOR LONGE-VITALITY

While the AC/DC frontman likely didn't have kombucha or green tea in mind, his dark humour alludes to a truth often missed in the fast-paced world of modern wellness: what we consume daily is both our poison and our potion. Nutrition doesn't merely feed the body; it shapes the trajectory of our vitality. From cellular renewal to disease resistance, from bone strength to brain function, the foods we choose, or refuse, write the script of our ageing story.

In this chapter, we explore how anti-inflammatory, traditional, and well-timed eating patterns can extend not just lifespan, but also healthspan. From cutting-edge *Longe-Vitality* science to the wisdom of ancient cultures, the evidence is mounting – we can quite literally eat for a long, vital life.

THE POWER OF ANTI-INFLAMMATORY DIETS

At the heart of healthy ageing lies the battle against chronic, low-grade inflammation. Unlike acute inflammation – a healing response to injury or infection – chronic inflammation silently erodes health over time, fuelling diseases like diabetes, cardiovascular illness, cancer, and cognitive decline.

Enter the Mediterranean diet, a time-honoured nutritional template steeped in olive oil, leafy greens, legumes, nuts, herbs, oily fish, and a moderate amount of wine. More than a trend, this diet has earned scientific validation. A comprehensive 2025 study found significantly reduced instances of rheumatoid arthritis among those following the Mediterranean model – huge news for the millions of people at risk of developing the condition as they age.[1]

One of the most influential proponents of this dietary pattern is Valter Longo, Italian-American biochemist and author of *The Longevity Diet*. Longo's research blends molecular gerontology with the traditional foodways of Southern Italy. His fasting-mimicking diet (FMD), a periodic, plant-based, calorie-restricted protocol, aims to reboot metabolism and promote autophagy: cellular cleaning and renewal.[2] In modern trials, FMD cycles have shown promise in reducing inflammation, boosting immune function, and even extending lifespan.[3]

Longo doesn't claim to have invented anything new. His best advice: "Eat at the table of your ancestors."[4] Indeed, many of the world's longest-lived people eat modestly, mostly plants, and practise cultural restraint around food. They don't eat until they're full – they stop just before.

HARA HACHI BU:
THE JAPANESE SECRET TO MODERATION

As mentioned in our Blue Zones discussion, in Okinawa, Japan, the phrase *hara hachi bu* is recited like a quiet blessing before meals. It translates to: "Eat until you are 80 percent full." This isn't a fad diet, but a centuries-old Confucian teaching woven into daily life. Many older Okinawans have embodied this principle for decades, pausing before satiety, eating mindfully, and treating food as both nourishment and medicine.

The benefits of *hara hachi bu* are borne out in science. By avoiding caloric excess, the practice helps prevent obesity, lowers oxidative stress, and supports metabolic health.[5] It mirrors the findings of calorie-restriction studies in humans, which show improved markers of cardiovascular, cognitive, and immune function without malnutrition.[6]

Misao Okawa, a Japanese supercentenarian who lived to 117, famously credited her longevity to sleep and sushi.[7] Her diet reflected a broader Japanese nutritional pattern: abundant fish rich in omega-3 fatty acids, seasonal vegetables, fermented foods such as miso and natto, and minimal processed sugar. This pattern is associated with lower rates of heart disease, dementia, and certain cancers.[8]

Unlike many Western dietary frameworks that emphasise strict restriction, calorie counting, or macronutrient ratios, the traditional Japanese approach celebrates balance and diversity. Meals often include at least five colours on the plate, encouraging a wide spectrum of micronutrients. A simple bento box may contain grilled fish, pickled vegetables, simmered greens, a small portion of rice, and fresh fruit, each in modest quantities. This variety not only nourishes the body, but also provides sensory satisfaction, reducing the drive to overeat.

Hara hachi bu isn't about scarcity; it's about sufficiency. It allows space for digestion, fosters appreciation for the meal, and aligns with broader Okinawan habits of daily movement, social connection, and purpose. It's a reminder that how we eat matters as much as what we eat, and that moderation isn't deprivation, but liberation from excess.

HYDRATION: THE UNSUNG HERO OF HEALTHY AGEING

Food often grabs the headlines in the conversation on healthy ageing – superfoods, anti-inflammatory diets, and the latest nutritional trends dominate our feeds. Yet water, the most fundamental nutrient of all, quietly works behind the scenes, often overlooked, yet arguably just as vital for sustaining a long, vibrant life.

In a landmark 2024 study, researchers found that those with optimal hydration were biologically younger, less likely to develop age-related diseases, and more likely to live well into older age.[9] Essentially, staying hydrated throughout the day is one of the simplest and most effective *Longe-Vitality* hacks available.

Why does water matter so much? It's the silent courier of life, delivering nutrients to our cells, flushing toxins, maintaining temperature balance, cushioning joints, and keeping our minds sharp. Even mild dehydration can reduce kidney efficiency, raise inflammatory markers, and accelerate biological ageing.[10] Over time, these small deficits compound, nudging the body towards decline.

As we age, the challenge grows. The natural perception of thirst diminishes, meaning older adults may not feel the urge to drink until dehydration is already setting in. This makes conscious hydration – meaning, not just drinking when thirsty – a critical longevity habit. General recommendations suggest around 2.6 litres (11 cups) per day for women and 3.5 litres (15 cups) for men, including water from food sources like fruit, vegetables, soups, and herbal teas. Endurance athletes, those in hot climates, and individuals with certain health conditions may need even more.[11]

In the *Longe-Vitality* philosophy, hydration isn't a checklist item; it's a daily ritual of self-preservation. Just as regular movement strengthens our cardiovascular system and balanced nutrition fuels our cells, water keeps the entire machine humming. Picture it as the river that flows through every organ and tissue, carrying vitality to the farthest reaches of the body.

The truth is simple but profound: in the quiet act of pouring a glass of water, we're making a micro-investment in our future self. The dividends, measured in sharper cognition, resilient joints, and an extra decade of vitality, are well worth the habit.

NUTRIENT TIMING: EAT WITH THE SUN

For decades, the conversation around nutrition has been dominated by what we eat, yet science is now revealing an equally vital layer: *when* we eat. This is the realm of chrononutrition, the study of how meal timing interacts with our circadian rhythms, the internal 24-hour clock that governs nearly every aspect of physiology.

Our circadian system orchestrates digestion, hormone release, glucose metabolism, and even the activity of our mitochondria, the tiny power plants in our cells. These rhythms evolved under predictable cycles of light and darkness, feast and fast. When we eat in sync with daylight, we work with our biology. When we graze late into the night, we create a form of 'metabolic jet lag', disrupting the natural ebb and flow of insulin sensitivity, fat metabolism, and cellular repair.

Late-night eating is particularly problematic. After sunset, melatonin rises, signalling the body to rest, not digest.

Metabolism slows, insulin sensitivity drops, and the likelihood of excess calories being stored as fat increases.[12] The result is a subtle but persistent shift towards weight gain, inflammation, and reduced metabolic flexibility.

In contrast, front-loading calories earlier in the day, when insulin sensitivity is naturally highest, has been shown to optimise blood sugar control, improve lipid profiles, and support healthier weight regulation. A landmark 2013 study confirmed that people who eat more of their daily energy at breakfast and lunch, rather than dinner, achieve better metabolic outcomes regardless of total calorie intake.[13]

One practical application of this science is time-restricted eating (TRE), a form of intermittent fasting where food is consumed within a set daily window, often 8 to 12 hours. A 2020 study found that when people practise TRE, they experience improved blood pressure, better insulin responses, reduced oxidative stress, and lower inflammation, without deliberate calorie restriction.[14]

The wisdom here is as ancient as it is modern. Our grandparents often 'ate with the sun', not because of controlled trials, but because life followed the rhythm of day and night. In your *Longe-Vitality* journey, this principle becomes a gentle but powerful nudge: finish your last meal before darkness falls. Let your evenings be for rest, not digestion. Your cells, your metabolism, and your waistline will thank you.

TEA FOR TWO? POLYPHENOLS AND THE POWER OF PLANTS

In many of the world's celebrated longevity hotspots, meals don't end with a rich slice of cake, but with a humble cup of tea. From the mist-kissed hills of Fujian to the high terraces of Yunnan, traditional Chinese teas, green, oolong, *pu-erh*, are steeped not only in centuries of culture, but also in a growing body of science. These teas are abundant in polyphenols, particularly catechins, which are potent antioxidants that counter oxidative stress, the biochemical 'rust' that erodes our cells over time. By neutralising free radicals and reducing cellular damage, these plant compounds support healthier ageing from the inside out.

Polyphenols also support endothelial function, helping blood vessels remain supple, modulate gut microbiota, which plays a role in inflammation and immunity, and may even influence neural plasticity, enhancing the brain's ability to adapt and maintain cognitive health in later life.[15] In fact, habitual tea drinkers have consistently been shown to perform better on cognitive tests, even after controlling for education and other lifestyle factors.[16]

In China, tea has long been considered a form of daily medicine, consumed not in isolation, but as part of a lifestyle rooted in mindful eating, social connection, and active movement. In the West, tea may be marketed as a health trend, but the truth is far older: a warm cup of polyphenol-rich leaves might be one of the most affordable, accessible, and culturally adaptable longevity tonics we have.

So, the next time you share a pot of tea, whether with a friend, a parent, or simply with yourself, remember – you're participating in a tradition that has quietly been adding quality years to human lives for millennia.

REAL-LIFE INSPIRATIONS: FC AND SL WONG

My own grandmothers, FC Wong and SL Wong, lived by dietary rhythms that modern research would applaud. Meals were almost entirely home-cooked, with a foundation of vegetables, legumes, rice, and modest portions of meat or fish. Soups that simmered for hours with goji berries, rich in carotenoids and polysaccharides associated with immune modulation, were commonplace. Chrysanthemum tea, consumed daily, contained flavonoids that may reduce oxidative stress and blood pressure.[17] In their eyes, these weren't 'functional foods'; they were simply the flavours of home.

Steamed greens such as bok choy, kai lan, and spinach provided folate, vitamin C, and calcium, while fermented condiments added probiotic diversity. Rice porridge (congee) was a breakfast staple, light, hydrating, and easy on digestion, often accompanied by pickled vegetables or a sprinkle of sesame seeds. The combination created meals that were anti-inflammatory by default, long before the term became fashionable.

Just as important as the nutrients was the context. Meals were shared with family, with laughter punctuating the clatter of chopsticks. Gratitude was expressed not just for the food, but for the company. For my grandmothers, this was simply life.

These lived examples highlight a core *Longe-Vitality* principle: nutrition isn't just biochemistry; it's culture, rhythm, and relationship. My grandmothers' soups were anchored in tradition and embedded in a lifestyle that values nourishment over novelty. They avoided the extremes that dominate modern diet culture and instead embraced a quiet consistency.

Current science affirms what my grandmothers practised intuitively: diets high in whole plant foods, rich in diverse phytochemicals, and low in ultra-processed ingredients are strongly associated with reduced risk of chronic disease and longer lifespan. The anti-inflammatory effects of polyphenols, carotenoids, and omega-3 fatty acids work synergistically to protect the cardiovascular system, preserve cognitive function, and maintain metabolic health well into old age.

The takeaway is clear: fuelling for *Longe-Vitality* isn't about chasing the next superfood trend, nor about rigidly tracking every gram of macronutrients. It's about building a foundation of whole, minimally processed foods, eaten in balance, and enjoyed in community. It's about food as both sustenance and story, linking generations through shared recipes and rituals. And perhaps most importantly, it's about consistency, because the magic of these dietary patterns emerges not over weeks or months, but over decades.

When culture supports health, *Longe-Vitality* is no accident. It becomes an inheritance.

RUN DOC'S LONGE-VITALITY TIPS

1

Embrace an anti-inflammatory diet.
Fuel longevity from the inside out. Fill your plate with antioxidant-rich foods: berries, leafy greens, turmeric, legumes, and extra-virgin olive oil. Cut back on refined carbs and added sugars that fan the flames of inflammation. Eat colourful. Eat clean. Eat for life.

2

Hydrate like your life depends on it – because it does.
Your cells are mostly water. Don't wait until thirst strikes. Sip steadily throughout the day, and elevate hydration with herbal teas such as chrysanthemum, green tea, or rooibos – nature's quiet elixirs for recovery and clarity.

3

Eat with the clock, not against it.
Timing is everything. Front-load your meals and eat lightly at dinner. An eating window – say, 8 am to 6 pm – that aligns with daylight hours supports metabolism, sleep, and hormonal balance. Let your rhythm mirror the sun.

4

Eat until 80 percent full.
Practise hara hachi bu, the Okinawan secret of mindful moderation. Chew slowly. Savour texture, flavour, gratitude. Stop before you're full – your gut, brain, and future self will thank you for the restraint.

5

Honour food culture.
Longevity begins at the family table. Return to tradition: Italian minestrone, Chinese congee, Japanese miso soup – humble, wholefood meals seasoned with generations of wisdom. Modern science finally agrees: our ancestors knew best.

EAT TO THRIVE, NOT JUST TO SURVIVE

Longe-Vitality isn't just about living long; it's about staying vibrant while you do. Nutrition, done right, empowers us to run marathons in our 70s, climb stairs without gasping, and dance at our great-grandchild's wedding.

And no, you don't need to sip embalming fluid to get there. Just pour yourself a warm cup of tea, plate up some plants, eat with the sun, and remember the wisdom of the long-lived: eat simply, live gratefully, and never underestimate the power of a good meal shared.

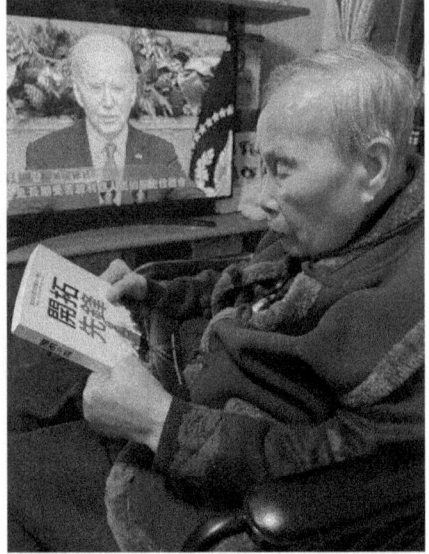

Presenting my PhD thesis and certificate to my late mother Demi

F Leung RIP 101 years old reading Trailblazing (Chinese edition)

With my now 97 year old grandma "Porpor" SL Wong

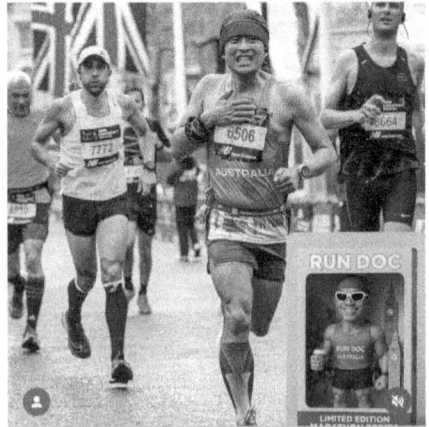

Current lifetime marathon PB at 2023 London Marathon

Helping to pace my daughter and son at HOKA half marathon

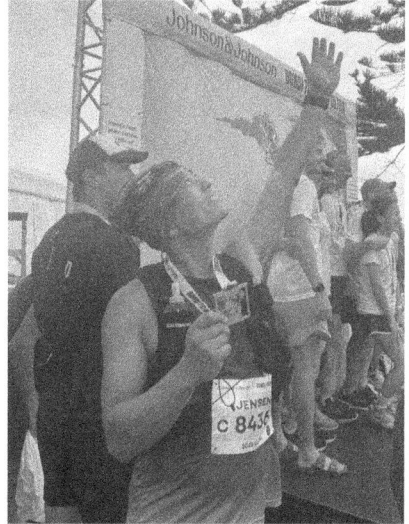
2025 Bondi-to-Manly Ultramarathon (80km) at the finish line, Manly Beach, raising my hand to the heavens to my late mother

At the start line of 2025 Berlin Marathon with my mates Nicki and Jennie (Jennie Kellett @runningfromoldage)

At work 2025

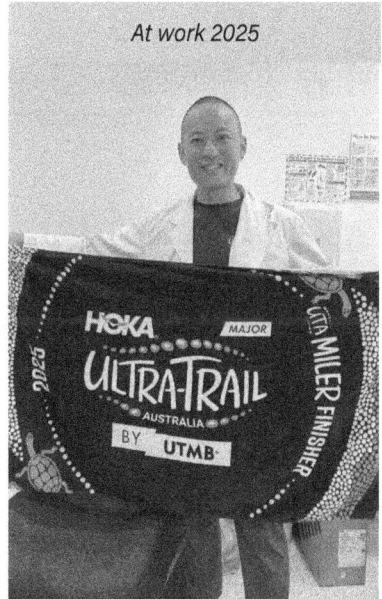

CHAPTER 8

THE SOUL OF RUNNING

FINDING JOY AND PURPOSE

"The mystery of human existence lies not in just staying alive, but in finding something to live for."

– Fyodor Dostoyevsky

THE SOURCE OF TRUE VITALITY

In the great quest for *Longe-Vitality*, many turn first to the physical: VO2 max, heart rate variability, lean muscle mass, anti-inflammatory diets. But true vitality, the kind that endures across decades, rarely originates solely in the body. It begins in the soul.

More than any supplement or statin, it's a sense of joy and purpose that sustains us. This soul fuel – the belief that your life has meaning and your movement serves something greater – is a critical yet often overlooked determinant of long, vital living. It's also the invisible thread linking people who not only age well, but live also fully.

This chapter explores movement not just as medicine, but as meaning. It's about the run as ritual, the walk as witness, and the dance as devotion. It's about finding joy in motion, and purpose in every step.

HARNESS THE POWER OF THE 'WHY TREE'

In *Trailblazing*, I shared a simple visual that has anchored countless runners navigating the storms of fatigue, injury, or self-doubt: the 'Why Tree'.

It begins underground, in the quiet strength of roots – your deepest values. These roots may be family, freedom, faith, or the belief that life should be lived in full stride rather than cautious half-steps. Above ground rises the trunk – your goals – firm, visible, and measurable: completing a first marathon, lowering blood pressure, staying fit enough to chase grandchildren. Then, stretching towards the sky, the branches represent your daily actions: pre-dawn runs, mindful meals, restorative sleep, and stretching sessions that keep both muscles supple and spirits high.

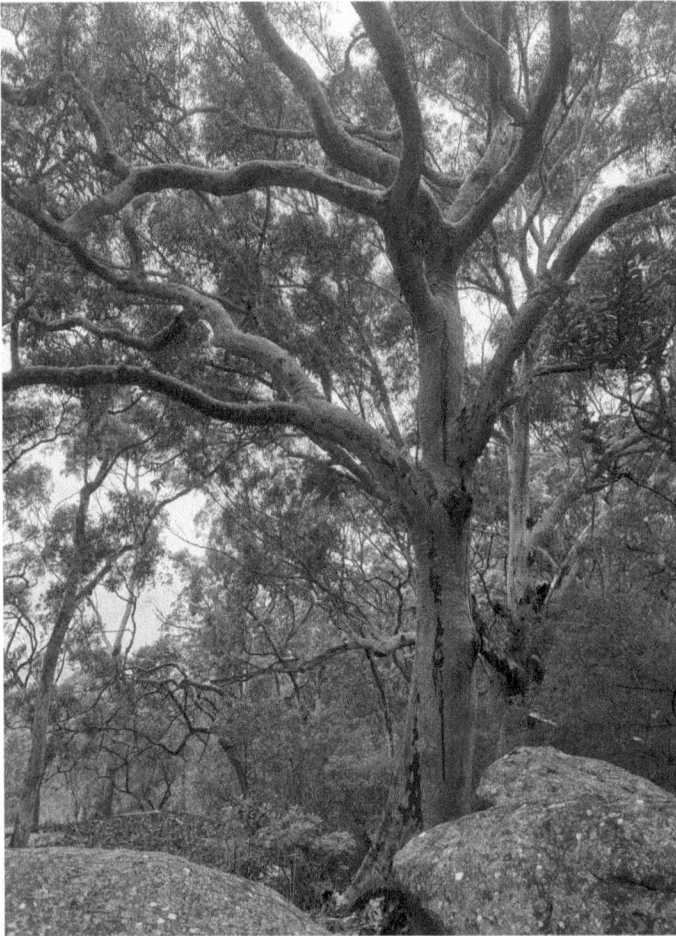

When runners hit the proverbial wall, I invite them to pause and 'see' their Why Tree. The roots remind them of foundation; the trunk holds them steady, and the branches show that growth happens one small leaf at a time. In moments of exhaustion, this reframing shifts the inner dialogue from *I can't* to *I will – because it matters.*

But here's the hidden layer: a Why Tree can't thrive on purpose alone. Just as a tree needs water, sunlight, and fertile soil, purpose-driven actions need the right fuel. In longevity science, this means optimising nutrition not just for the next race, but for vitality over decades. Purpose without nourishment will wither; nourishment without purpose will lack direction. Together, they create the synergy that sustains a long, vital life.

From a biological perspective, purposeful living and nutrient-rich diets work hand in hand. Studies show that having a strong sense of purpose is linked to lower risks of cardiovascular events and premature mortality, independent of traditional risk factors.[1] As we know, diets abundant in plant-based whole foods – rich in phytonutrients, omega-3 fatty acids, and anti-inflammatory compounds – are consistently associated with increased lifespan and reduced chronic disease burden.

When fuelling for longevity, I encourage athletes to imagine feeding their roots. Foods that nourish at the cellular level – deep-green leafy vegetables, brightly coloured berries, nuts, seeds, and legumes – are the soil that sustains both body and purpose. These provide antioxidants that reduce oxidative stress, slowing telomere attrition and supporting DNA repair.[2] High-quality proteins – wild-caught fish, pastured eggs, or plant-based sources like lentils and tofu – form the sturdy fibres of the trunk, preserving muscle mass and metabolic resilience well into older age.

Hydration is the water that keeps branches supple. Adequate fluid intake supports cellular resilience, cognitive clarity, and cardiovascular efficiency. For endurance runners, strategic fuelling also matters: carbohydrate intake before and during long runs maintains glycogen stores, prevents central fatigue, and keeps pace sustainable. Post-run, replenishing with protein plus complex carbohydrates accelerates recovery, reduces soreness, and prepares the body for the next growth phase.

The 'fertiliser' for your Why Tree shouldn't be ultra-processed foods. Diets dominated by refined sugars, industrial seed oils, and processed meats degrade the soil, fuelling systemic inflammation, arterial stiffness, and metabolic decline. Contrast that with the Mediterranean and Okinawan eating patterns – rich in polyphenols, healthy fats, unrefined carbohydrates – which help centenarians live not only longer, but with remarkable functional independence.

Importantly, the Why Tree isn't static – it's seasonal. There will be times of vigorous growth, times of pruning, and times of rest. The key is to keep the roots nourished through daily lifestyle choices so the trunk stays strong and the branches continue reaching. Fuelling with purpose isn't about perfection, but about alignment. When nutrition supports training, and training serves your deepest values, you create a self-reinforcing cycle: purpose fuels performance; performance sustains purpose.

So next time you lace up for a run or sit down for a meal, ask yourself: Am I feeding my roots, or depleting them? Over years and decades, that answer shapes not just how long your tree stands, but how wide its shade stretches.

SATISH KUMAR: THE PILGRIM'S PATH

In the 1960s, Satish Kumar, a former Jain monk turned peace activist, undertook a journey that defied both convention and common sense. Alongside fellow pilgrim EP Menon, Satish walked from his home in India to the capitals of the world's four nuclear powers – Moscow, Paris, London, and Washington, DC – a distance of over 13,000 kilometres. He carried no money, accepted no paid transport, and relied entirely on the kindness of strangers for food and shelter.[3]

Why? Because for Satish, walking wasn't merely about getting from A to B. It was a spiritual statement. His journey was a prayer in motion – a declaration that peace can't be delivered by bombs, only by the deliberate steps of human connection. His only luggage was a small bundle of essentials and a heart anchored in a single conviction: his body, his feet, his journey were his instruments of change.

The walk took over 2 years, traversing deserts, mountains, and war-torn regions. At every stop, Satish spoke of peace, compassion, and the need for humanity to tread more lightly on the Earth. The absence of money was intentional: it stripped away the false securities of modern life, forcing reliance on human kindness, shared meals, and the reciprocity of trust. Each step became an act of faith, each encounter a reminder of our shared humanity.

Now in his late 80s, Satish continues to walk daily. For him, walking isn't merely locomotion – it's locomeditation.[4] His pace is slow, but his presence is profound. In a world that chases speed, Satish embodies stillness in motion.

From a longevity perspective, Satish's story is more than philosophical; it's biological. As we know, walking is one of the most accessible forms of physical activity, proven to reduce cardiovascular risk, improve cognitive function, and enhance emotional wellbeing. Even low-intensity, consistent walking has been linked with lower all-cause mortality.[5] But for Satish, the act of walking transcends physical health. It nourishes the psyche, strengthens the spirit, and grounds the soul.

Science now affirms what pilgrims, monks, and long-distance runners have long known: moving with intention alters our brain chemistry. Rhythmic, moderate-intensity movement – whether walking or running – stimulates endorphin release, boosts serotonin, and promotes neuroplasticity.[6] This is why so many endurance athletes describe a meditative 'flow state' during long efforts. Satish's 'locomeditation' is, in essence, an ancient form of this flow – untethered from competition, anchored in purpose.

His life invites us to reimagine movement as an act of service. He walked for peace. Others might run to raise funds for clean water, or walk with a grieving friend, or run to deliver life-saving medicine in rural areas. The purpose is personal, but the principle is universal: movement can be more than self-improvement; it can be a vehicle for collective healing.

As runners, we often measure success in kilometres logged, paces achieved, and medals earned. Satish offers a gentler metric: measure your movement by the depth of connection it brings – to yourself, to others, and to the Earth beneath your feet. When movement becomes a dialogue rather than a monologue, when we listen with our feet, we begin to touch the soul of running.

When it comes to *Longe-Vitality*, the lesson is clear. Purpose amplifies the benefits of physical activity. When our running or walking is infused with meaning beyond personal gain, the psychological and physiological rewards multiply. Satish's pilgrimage reminds us that the longest journeys aren't measured in miles, but in the transformations they spark, within us and around us.

THE SCIENCE OF PURPOSE

As the Run Doc, I've seen firsthand how a deep 'why' can transform not only an athlete's performance but also their health trajectory. Purpose gets you out the door on the days you'd rather stay in bed. Purpose keeps you lacing up long after the novelty wears off.

As discussed in chapter two, science now shows that purpose reaches all the way down to your cells, significantly reducing all-cause mortality. Purpose isn't just a companion to good health; it's an independent driver, acting as a biological buffer against life's inevitable storms.

The power of purpose partly lies in inflammation. Research has linked purpose to lower levels of interleukin-6 (IL-6), a key inflammatory cytokine associated with cardiovascular disease, cancer, and accelerated ageing.[7] Lower IL-6 levels translate into reduced chronic inflammation, better immune regulation, and slower cellular wear and tear.

For runners, this isn't an abstract theory; it's lived reality.

Purpose is what keeps the ultramarathoner moving through the cold, dark hours before dawn. It's what powers the weekend runner to show up for a charity event that funds cancer research. In those moments, every step is a micro-act of alignment between values and action.

And there's a feedback loop: running with purpose often deepens purpose itself. The rhythm of movement becomes a meditation, a chance to strip life back to its essentials. You discover that your run isn't just about kilometres or finish times; it's about becoming the kind of person who honours commitments, embraces challenge, and finds joy in service.

From a longevity perspective, this matters. Purposeful runners aren't simply logging miles; they're weaving meaning into their physiology. Every training session is an act of cellular signalling: to the heart, *Stay strong*; to the immune system, *Stay balanced*; to the mind, *Stay hopeful*. In the long run – quite literally – it's not only your VO2 max or lactate threshold that determines how far you'll go. It's also the size of your 'why'.

HARRIETTE THOMPSON: JOY IN EVERY STEP

At age 76, Harriette Thompson laced up for her first marathon. Sixteen years later, at 92, she became the oldest woman to complete the distance, crossing the finish line of the Rock 'n' Roll San Diego Marathon with a smile that seemed to defy both the clock and conventional biology.

A classically trained concert pianist, Harriette approached running with the same grace, rhythm, and discipline that music had taught her. But she didn't run to prove anything about age. She ran because she loved life, and because every stride carried meaning. Each marathon she entered became a moving fundraiser for cancer research, a cause woven into her personal story. She had survived oral cancer, endured radiation, and lost loved ones to the disease.[8] Running wasn't simply exercise; it was her way of transforming grief into generosity, hardship into hope. Her marathon was a 42-kilometre hymn – not to speed, but to resilience.

Harriette's mindset aligns perfectly with what psychologists call eudaimonic wellbeing – the sense of fulfilment that comes from living with purpose. With research consistently linking this kind of meaning-driven life to lower inflammation, better immune function, and reduced mortality risk, her joy wasn't just an attitude; it was a physiological advantage.

Harriette's story is a masterclass in longevity through movement. She embodies three critical principles:

1. Run for something bigger than yourself – purpose sustains effort far beyond what willpower alone can achieve.

2. Measure success in meaning, not minutes – pace fades; purpose persists.

3. See yourself as ageless in action – identity shapes biology, influencing how we age from the inside out.

In a culture obsessed with finish times and personal bests, Harriette reminds us that the deepest victories aren't measured on a stopwatch. They're found in the moments when movement becomes an act of love – for ourselves, for others, for life itself. Her life poses the question: What would you run for if you knew you could inspire someone else to take their first step? Because as Harriette proved, joy in every step isn't just a philosophy. It's a path to a longer, fuller, more vital life.

RUNNING AS SACRED RITUAL

Movement becomes ritual when it's infused with intention. It's no longer just exercise; it's an offering – to ourselves, to others, and to the life we wish to live. For many runners, this transformation happens in the stillness of a sunrise trail.

The air is cool, the light new, and the soundscape reduced to birdsong and breath. The body falls into its rhythm – footfalls, inhalation, exhalation – and the mind begins to soften, unclenching from the noise of the day before.

It's *flow,* that elusive yet unmistakable state when effort dissolves into ease, when pace ceases to matter, and presence takes centre stage. It's when you're not chasing distance or data; you're simply there, experiencing the moment. Physiologists may measure it as a balance of dopamine, serotonin, and endorphins, but lived experience tells us it's something deeper – an alignment of body, mind, and spirit.

Running can be so much more than sport. In a study of ultramarathoners, elite and recreational alike described running as a form of self-transcendence – a vehicle to connect to nature, to community, and to something ineffable beyond themselves.[9] When you approach each run not as a task to complete but as a ritual to inhabit, you engage more fully with the present moment.

Purpose-driven movement also changes your physiology. Research suggests that people who exercise with intrinsic motivation – driven by enjoyment, meaning, and personal values – have greater adherence and more sustained health benefits than those motivated by appearance or obligation.[10] In other words, the joy is the discipline.

When I run, I think of my grandmothers. I think of their quiet, purposeful movement and how it shaped not only their longevity but their capacity for connection. Running has become my way of honouring them, each step a reminder that health isn't just about adding years to life, but life to years.

So lace up – not just to train, but to attune. Let the road, the trail, or the park path become your temple. In the act of running, you may just discover that the sacred isn't somewhere else – it's right here, in the rhythm of your breath and the beating of your heart.

MOVEMENT AS EXPRESSION, NOT OBLIGATION

Too often, movement is framed as a debt to be repaid – burn calories, shed weight, earn your rest. This mindset turns something inherently human into a transaction, draining it of joy. But what if we reclaimed movement as an act of expression, not penance?

Think of a child running barefoot in the park – they're not calculating their heart rate or wondering how many kilometres they've logged. They're simply expressing the fact that they're alive. Somewhere along the way, adulthood teaches us to measure, justify, and commodify movement, but we can choose a different narrative. You can dance not to 'burn off' dessert, but because the music moves you. You can walk not to meet a step goal, but because the sunrise invites you. You can run not because you must, but because you're called to explore, to serve, to celebrate. When movement reflects your values, it becomes something deeper than habit. If your values include service, you might run to raise funds for a cause. If they include creativity, you might find inspiration for your art while moving through nature. If they include courage, you might sign up for a race that scares you, knowing the training will shape you in ways the finish line never could. This shift matters because joy sustains. Discipline may get you started, but delight keeps you going year after year. A training plan can keep you accountable, but a sense of purpose will get you out the door on the cold, dark mornings when your watch battery is flat and Strava won't record a thing.

At its best, movement isn't about fixing your body but inhabiting it fully. It's not about delaying death but deepening life. It's a daily reminder that you're capable, adaptable, and gloriously alive. And so, the soul of running – of any movement – isn't found in the stopwatch or the scales, but in the truth it whispers back to you: you are here. You are moving. You are free.

RUN DOC'S LONGE-VITALITY TIPS

1

Move with meaning.
Choose movement that mirrors your values and nourishes your spirit. Run to clear your mind. Walk to connect with nature. Stretch to slow down and listen inwardly. Longevity begins when every step has purpose.

2

Create rituals, not just routines.
A ritual transforms repetition into reverence. Begin each session with a word of gratitude, a prayer, or a deep breath. End with reflection – What did this movement mean today? Rituals anchor your body to your soul.

3

Link goals to identity.
Trade hollow goals for meaningful ones. Instead of saying, "I want to lose five kilos," say, "I run to stay strong for my children" or, "I move so I can serve others with energy and joy." When purpose fuels performance, progress lasts.

4

Build a purpose-driven community.
Surround yourself with people who share your deeper why. Join a run club with a cause, a walking group through your faith community, or a volunteering team that moves for good. Purpose multiplies when shared.

5

Let purpose evolve.
Purpose isn't fixed; it matures with you. Run for competition in your 30s, for contemplation in your 50s, for connection in your 70s. Be curious about who you're becoming. The long run of life isn't about pace – it's about purpose.

PURPOSE IS NON-NEGOTIABLE

Purpose isn't optional. It's as vital to the ageing process as movement, sleep, and nutrition. It's the soul of *Longe-Vitality*, the spark that gets us up, the fuel that keeps us going, the compass that helps us endure. Whether you're a nun running marathons in your 80s, a peace pilgrim walking across continents, or a concert pianist lacing up at 90, your movement can carry sacred weight.

You may never race an Ironman. You may never walk from India to Washington. But you can live, move, and breathe with purpose. So run for something. Walk for someone. Move for some reason that makes your heart beat stronger than your feet. And in doing so, you'll not only live longer; you'll live better. One step. One breath. One sacred act of joy and purpose at a time.

CHAPTER 9

THE RESILIENT MINDSET

OVERCOMING AGE AND ADVERSITY

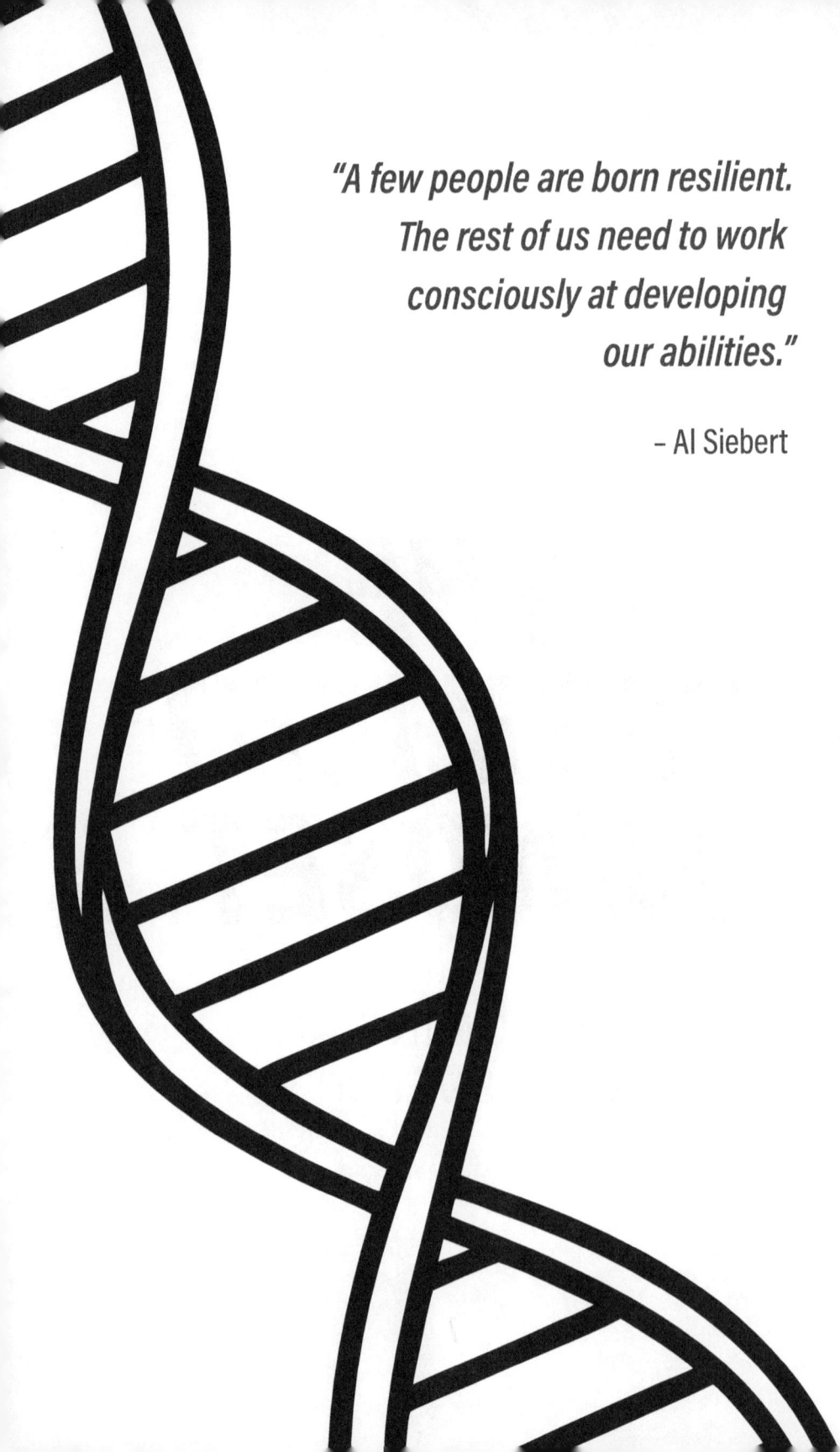

"A few people are born resilient. The rest of us need to work consciously at developing our abilities."

– Al Siebert

AGE WITH RESILIENCE AND GRACE

We often think of ageing as a purely physical process – a gradual erosion of muscle strength, stamina, and mobility. Yet, when you observe those who age vibrantly, you notice a different defining factor. Beneath the surface, what truly separates those who flourish from those who merely endure is something quieter but infinitely more powerful: the capacity to adapt – mentally, emotionally, and spiritually – to life's inevitable changes and challenges. This is the essence of resilience and, by extension, *Longe-Vitality*.

Resilience isn't the denial of difficulty; it's the alchemy of using adversity as a catalyst for growth. It's the inner steadiness that allows a person recovering from surgery to re-enter their walking routine sooner, the determination that propels a widow to join a new community group, or the optimism that fuels a masters athlete to train for another race despite an injury. In later life, this trait becomes the silent engine that powers recovery after illness, keeps us active after setbacks, and allows us to 'bounce forward', not merely back, when the road gets rough.

Science supports the notion that resilience isn't fixed; it can be cultivated. Research from the Harvard Study of Adult Development – the longest-running longitudinal study of ageing – found that the ability to maintain positive relationships and adapt to life's stressors is strongly linked to both healthspan and lifespan.[1]

Much like building muscle, developing resilience requires consistent, intentional practice. This can take the form of reframing challenges as opportunities, practising mindfulness to anchor ourselves in the present, fostering supportive social networks, and setting small but meaningful goals. Physical activity itself plays a surprisingly potent role. Endurance running, hiking, and other regular movement-based pursuits not only condition the body but also repeatedly expose the mind to manageable doses of discomfort and uncertainty, building mental toughness over time.

Resilience is also intertwined with a sense of purpose. Viktor Frankl, the Holocaust survivor and psychiatrist, observed that those who could find meaning – even in suffering – were more likely to endure.[2] In longevity terms, having a reason to get up in the morning isn't just psychologically protective; it may influence biological ageing through hormonal, immune, and neural pathways. That's right – as research increasingly reveals, developing a resilient mindset doesn't just help us cope; it might just help us live longer.

ED WHITLOCK: THE CEMETERY RUNNER

If Sister Madonna Buder's story speaks to purpose and spirituality, Ed Whitlock's life is a masterclass in grit, solitude, and the relentless testing of limits – proof that the mind can carry the body far beyond what age would suggest.

Ed, a retired mining engineer from Canada, quietly rewrote the record books. In 2003, at the age of 72, he became the first person over 70 to run a marathon in under 3 hours – a feat so improbable that sports scientists had to double-check the timing mats. But he didn't stop there. At 85, he completed the 2016 Toronto Waterfront Marathon in 3:56:38, setting an age-group world record that still leaves physiologists shaking their heads.[3]

It wasn't just the numbers that made him remarkable; it was how he achieved them. Ed eschewed sports science labs, structured intervals, and high-tech gear. Instead, he trained alone, often for 3 hours at a time, circling the same cemetery near his home in Milton, Ontario.[4] No music. No watch obsession. No cheering crowds. Just the rhythm of his breath, the scrape of his shoes on gravel, and the unspoken agreement that he would return tomorrow. This wasn't eccentricity; it was discipline distilled to its purest form. Ed's approach embodied grit – the combination of passion and sustained perseverance towards long-term goals. In ageing populations, grit and mental resilience have been linked not only to athletic performance, but also to better health outcomes, lower rates of depression, and slower cognitive decline.[5]

Ed's solitary cemetery loops were also an exercise in voluntary discomfort, a trait common in resilient individuals. He didn't wait for perfect weather or an 'in the mood' day; he showed up, in snow, rain, and wind. This mindset, applied over decades, likely contributed to his remarkable longevity in the sport.

Ed's results reveal a powerful truth: with consistency, self-belief, and a willingness to train beyond comfort, the ageing curve can be bent – if not entirely broken.

His story also challenges our modern obsession with novelty and constant stimulation. In an era where fitness often comes packaged with apps, playlists, and 'gamified' metrics, Ed chose the monotony of repetition. That simplicity may have been his secret weapon. Repetitive, meditative training can strengthen not only the cardiovascular system, but also mental focus and emotional regulation.[6]

Ultimately, Ed's life is more than an inspirational footnote in marathon history. It's a blueprint for resilience at any age. His training ground – a quiet cemetery – could be symbolic: a place that reminded him daily of mortality, yet fuelled his refusal to stop moving. Each lap was both a nod to life's brevity and a declaration that ageing, while inevitable, doesn't have to mean retreat.

Resilience, as Ed showed, is rarely glamorous. It's the decision to put on your shoes when you'd rather stay inside. It's enduring the quiet stretches where progress is invisible. It's finding purpose in the act itself, rather than the applause. And perhaps most importantly, it's having the courage to keep asking the question: What's still possible?

Ed answered that question not with speeches or slogans, but with thousands of silent, steady footsteps, proving that the strongest mindset may be the one that keeps showing up long after the crowd has gone home.

YUICHIRO MIURA: THE SUMMIT SEEKER

While Ed Whitlock's battleground was the flat, repetitive cemetery loop, Yuichiro Miura's was the thin, freezing air above 8,000 metres. Born in 1932 in Aomori, Japan, Yuichiro was already a legendary skier and adventurer when, in his 70s and 80s, he turned his sights to the world's highest mountain.

In 2003, at 70, he became the oldest person to summit Mount Everest. Most would have retired the crampons there. Instead, he returned at 75 and again at 80. Each ascent required years of preparation, not only to build physical strength but also to recover from serious health challenges, including two heart surgeries.[7]

Climbing Everest at any age is a crucible of resilience – extreme cold, thin air, dangerous crevasses, and the constant mental whisper to turn back. For an octogenarian, it requires something more: an unshakable belief that age isn't the final arbiter of possibility. Yuichiro's achievements highlight the importance of knowing when to conserve, when to push, and never fully conceding the summit of one's own potential.

Yuichiro's story is a living embodiment of this 'challenge hypothesis' of ageing, where adversity, when embraced with preparation and adaptability, becomes a driver of vitality.

ANGELA MADSEN: ROWING AGAINST THE CURRENT

In the world of endurance, resilience is often forged in the quiet miles and the unseen struggles. Few embodied this truth more powerfully than Angela Madsen, US Marine Corps veteran, Paralympic medallist, trans-Pacific rower, and relentless dream-chaser.

Her story began with promise and discipline, but a botched back surgery in her 20s left her paralysed from the waist down. In an instant, the physical identity she had built in the military was taken from her.[8] What followed was a cascade of hardship: homelessness, financial instability, chronic pain, and bouts of depression.[9] Where society saw limitation, Angela saw unfinished business.

She discovered adaptive rowing in the late 1990s – a sport that not only gave her a new outlet for her competitive spirit, but also re-anchored her sense of purpose. From there, her ambitions expanded beyond the boathouse. She crossed the Atlantic Ocean in a rowboat. She rowed the Indian Ocean. She competed in the Paralympics, winning bronze in London 2012.[10] And she kept asking herself: What else is possible?

At an age when most are thinking of slowing down, Angela set her sights on the Pacific – solo. She knew the dangers. She knew the statistics. But she also knew the rewards of living fully engaged, even in the face of risk. In June 2020, while attempting to row from California to Hawaii alone, she passed away at sea.[11] Friends and supporters were devastated, yet no one doubted this truth: Angela died doing precisely what she loved – pushing her limits on the open water.

Angela's mindset wasn't naive optimism. It was forged in the crucible of trauma, refined by years of battling systemic barriers and personal demons. She lived the mantra she often shared: on the bad days, "row harder."[12] In this way, she embodied what psychologists call post-traumatic growth, the phenomenon where adversity catalyses not just recovery, but a profound expansion of one's capacity and perspective.[13]

Her life also illustrates what longevity science increasingly confirms: mindset is a powerful determinant of both healthspan and resilience. Studies have found that people with higher optimism scores live longer and are more likely to achieve exceptional longevity – defined as living beyond 85 years – regardless of socio-economic or health status.[14] Optimism doesn't erase hardship, but it does shape the lens through which we navigate it, influencing stress responses, immune function, and even cardiovascular health.

Angela's story challenges the narrative that age and disability are endpoints. Instead, they can be turning points. In the *Longe-Vitality* framework, she is an exemplar of purpose-driven persistence – a mindset that fuels both physical endurance and life endurance. Her ocean crossings were more than feats of strength; they were declarations of autonomy over her own story.

We live in a culture that often underestimates older adults, particularly those with disabilities. Angela refused to be underestimated. She reframed her paralysis not as the end of her athletic identity, but as the beginning of a new chapter. This reframing aligns with cognitive-behavioural approaches that encourage identifying controllable factors, setting self-determined goals, and cultivating mastery over time. It's a strategy not just for sport, but also for ageing well.

In her final years, Angela trained daily, planned meticulously, and maintained an unwavering connection to her 'why'. For Angela, purpose wasn't abstract – it was tangible, mapped out on nautical charts and measured in nautical miles. Her story reminds us that resilience isn't the absence of fear or hardship. It's the decision – made again and again – to engage fully with life, no matter the weight of the waves.

THE WISDOM OF TWO GRANDMOTHERS

Closer to home, I grew up witnessing a different kind of resilience: quieter, but no less powerful. My two grandmothers never ran marathons or crossed oceans, but they navigated war, widowhood, poverty, and motherhood with astonishing tenacity. Their lives were living case studies in grit, adaptability, and the will to endure – principles as vital to healthy ageing as any exercise prescription or nutrition plan.

One of them [which one?], a mother of six, was widowed early. She raised her children through sheer determination and sacrifice, in a time and place where social support was minimal. I remember her hauling groceries up multiple flights of stairs with a toddler strapped to her back – her youngest grandson, Jeff – well into her 60s. She never once complained. Her strength was silent, but it was unshakable.

Both of my grandmothers consistently showed up – for their families, their communities, and their daily responsibilities. In modern terms, they cultivated psychological resilience, the capacity to adapt to life's challenges while maintaining a sense of purpose. This is the same quality that helps ultramarathoners push through the last gruelling miles or centenarians recover after a fall.

Resilience was woven into the fabric of their lives, not as a dramatic act of heroism, but as a daily choice. In the language of longevity science, they embodied the 'stress inoculation' principle, facing manageable, repeated challenges that built their capacity to withstand bigger ones later in life. Chronic stress, especially when perceived as unmanageable, accelerates biological ageing through mechanisms like telomere shortening and elevated cortisol.[15] But the kind of stress my grandmothers experienced – and reframed as meaningful – may have strengthened them.

This perspective is supported by research on eustress, or positive stress. In her book *The Upside of Stress,* Kelly McGonigal describes how reframing stress as a sign of engagement and purpose can transform its impact on health.[16] My widowed grandmother's load of groceries was heavy, but in her mind, it wasn't a burden – it was nourishment for her children.

My grandmothers also practised what modern psychologists call self-determined living. They made choices aligned with their values, despite external hardships. Self-determination theory suggests that autonomy, mastery, and relatedness – three psychological needs – are key to wellbeing and sustained motivation across our lifespans.[17] My grandmothers had all three, albeit without knowing the terminology.

Their stories remind me that the resilient mindset isn't about perfection or invincibility; it's about elasticity. It's the ability to bend without breaking, to adapt without losing yourself. And while resilience can be cultivated through training and habit, its most powerful expression is often found in the ordinary acts of everyday life.

As we consider how to age not just longer, but better, we would do well to remember that resilience doesn't always look like the cover of a sports magazine. Sometimes it's a pair of weathered hands tying a market bag. Sometimes it's carrying more than you thought you could —both literally and figuratively — because someone you love depends on it. And sometimes the most enduring marathons aren't measured in kilometres, but in the countless steps taken over a lifetime, in service of something greater than yourself.

THE SCIENCE OF RESILIENCE

Resilience is often thought of as a personal trait, a quiet strength that allows us to bend without breaking, but modern science is revealing that resilience is more than a psychological flourish. It's a biological ally, shaping how our bodies age and recover over time. In essence, the way we respond to life's inevitable challenges may be just as important for our healthspan as the nutrients we consume or the miles we run.

The research is compelling. A 2024 study that assessed older adults over a 4-year period found that those with higher psychological resilience scores had markedly lower all-cause mortality – even after adjusting for baseline health conditions.[18] Resilience didn't just make them feel better; it helped them live longer.

Resilience also plays a critical role in enhancing our quality of life as we age. A 2024 study found that psychological resilience can prevent and halt the progression of frailty.[19] Where others might succumb to the downward spiral of immobility and loss of confidence, resilient individuals are more likely to maintain activity levels, mobility, and strength.

The link between resilience and endurance isn't confined to clinical settings; it extends into the athletic arena. Research demonstrates that high levels of grit and resilience predict not only better athletic performance but also greater adherence to training regimens.[20] In other words, it's not just talent or youthful physiology that carries you across a marathon finish line. It's the ability to keep showing up, even when the weather, your legs, or your mood are working against you.

From a longevity perspective, resilience can be seen as a protective multiplier. It buffers the physiological stress response, dampens chronic inflammation, enhances recovery capacity, and promotes behaviours that, over time, compound like interest in a well-managed savings account. A setback – a fall, an injury, a diagnosis – becomes not a full stop, but a comma in the ongoing sentence of life.

Cultivating resilience isn't an act of wishful thinking but of deliberate practice. It can be nurtured through structured strategies: reframing challenges as opportunities for growth, engaging in regular physical activity (which itself boosts mood and stress tolerance), maintaining strong social connections, and setting purposeful goals that pull you forward. Just as muscles adapt to repeated load, our psychological resilience grows with repeated, intentional use.

In the end, ageing well isn't about eliminating adversity; it's about strengthening our capacity to navigate it. Resilience is the bridge between what happens to us and how well we live in the aftermath. It's a quiet, often invisible force that may be one of the most powerful longevity interventions we have at our disposal. And unlike many medical treatments, it's available to anyone willing to practise it daily.

In short, your mind doesn't just interpret your world; it shapes your biology.

TRAINING THE RESILIENT MIND

Resilience isn't a fixed trait you either have or don't. It's a dynamic skill set, one you can cultivate over a lifetime. Just as your hamstrings strengthen with repeated sprints, your mind fortifies through repeated challenge. Neuroscience shows that the brain's plasticity extends into our later decades, meaning it's never too late to become more mentally resilient.[21] The key is deliberate practice.

1. Visualisation – Rehearsing Victory Before It Arrives

Elite marathoners, Olympic divers, and NASA astronauts all share a common mental tool: visualisation. By vividly imagining yourself navigating a race's final kilometre, delivering a flawless presentation, or enduring a medical procedure, you activate neural circuits almost identical to those used in the actual act.[22] This mental simulation strengthens both confidence and emotional control. In running, I've used visualisation to 'pre-live' the discomfort of the 35 km mark in a marathon, when the body pleads for mercy but the mind must answer, *Not yet.*

2. Goal-Setting and Micro-Wins – the Psychology of Progress

The human brain is wired to respond to progress. Setting micro-goals – running 5 minutes longer than yesterday, walking one extra block, adding an extra rep – creates a positive feedback loop. Each win reinforces the belief, *I can adapt.* Research on behaviour change confirms that small, consistent achievements are more sustainable than radical overhauls.[23] In ageing athletes, micro-wins sustain motivation when peak performance is no longer a viable measure of success.

3. Reframing – from Decline to Refinement

Setbacks are inevitable: injuries, illnesses, changes in capacity. Resilient people master the art of reframing, transforming "why me?" into "what now?" Studies show that cognitive reappraisal not only reduces emotional distress but also strengthens long-term mental health.[24] Ageing can be viewed not as a loss but as a distillation, a refining of purpose and skill. In *Longe-Vitality*, we call this 'refining the blade' – sharpening the mental edge even if the body's steel softens.

4. Stress Inoculation – Training Under Pressure

Just as vaccines prepare the immune system by exposing it to a controlled threat, stress inoculation exposes the mind to manageable discomfort to build tolerance for adversity. Cold-water immersion, high-intensity intervals, and even deliberate public speaking challenges can strengthen your mental 'shock absorbers'.[25] For older athletes, controlled stress prevents overprotection, a common trap where avoidance of all discomfort accelerates both physical and cognitive decline.

5. Faith, Identity, and Community – Anchors in the Storm

Social connection is a robust predictor of resilience across all ages.[26] Whether anchored in a running club, a spiritual community, or a shared mission, these networks provide belonging and perspective. In my own journey, post-ultramarathon recovery is faster when surrounded by people who 'get it'. Likewise, centenarians in Blue Zones share strong communal bonds and a deep sense of purpose.

BUILDING RESILIENCE AS YOU AGE

Resilience training isn't about eliminating hardship but about expanding your capacity to face it. The research is clear: people who actively engage in resilience-building practices – visualisation, goal-setting, reframing, stress inoculation, and community engagement – maintain higher cognitive function, lower stress markers, and better overall health in later life.[27] For the runner, it means staying on the road despite injury; for the entrepreneur, it means pivoting when markets collapse; for the retiree, it means embracing life's next chapter with curiosity, not fear.

Your muscles don't strengthen by avoiding resistance; neither does your mind. Train it daily. Use it purposefully. And remember – resilience isn't about 'bouncing back' to who you were before. It's about bouncing forward into someone wiser, stronger, and more ready for the miles ahead.

RUN DOC'S LONGE-VITALITY TIPS

1

Train your brain like your body.
Mental fitness matters. Visualisation, journalling, and gratitude are just as essential as tempo runs and hill repeats. A strong mind sustains a strong stride.

2

Find meaning in movement.
Running isn't just cardio; it's connection. It can be prayer, play, protest, or purpose. Every step is a conversation between body, mind, and soul.

3

Progress over perfection.
Forget flawless. Choose consistent. Resilient runners show up on the hard days, when motivation fades but commitment carries them through.

4

Turn pain into perspective.
Injury, grief, and setbacks are teachers in disguise. Each challenge builds patience, humility, and wisdom – fuel for both longevity and life.

5

Connect to your 'why'.
Purpose powers endurance. When the road grows long and the miles get heavy, your why is what keeps you moving forward.

STRIDE TOWARDS RESILIENCE

Resilience isn't denial of hardship; it's defiance in the face of it. It's Sister Madonna crossing finish lines when others said she was too old. It's Ed Whitlock running laps in silence. It's Angela Madsen rowing across oceans. It's two grandmothers rising early, walking forward, and smiling through storms.

Whether you're 45 or 85, resilience is still within your reach. You don't have to be extraordinary; you just have to begin. Each day you show up with purpose, each time you take a step forward when it would be easier to stop, you're training not just your body, but your spirit. Let that be the heartbeat of your *Longe-Vitality* journey. Train it. Live it. Pass it on.

CHAPTER 10

COMMUNITIES OF LONGE-VITALITY

THE POWER OF CONNECTION

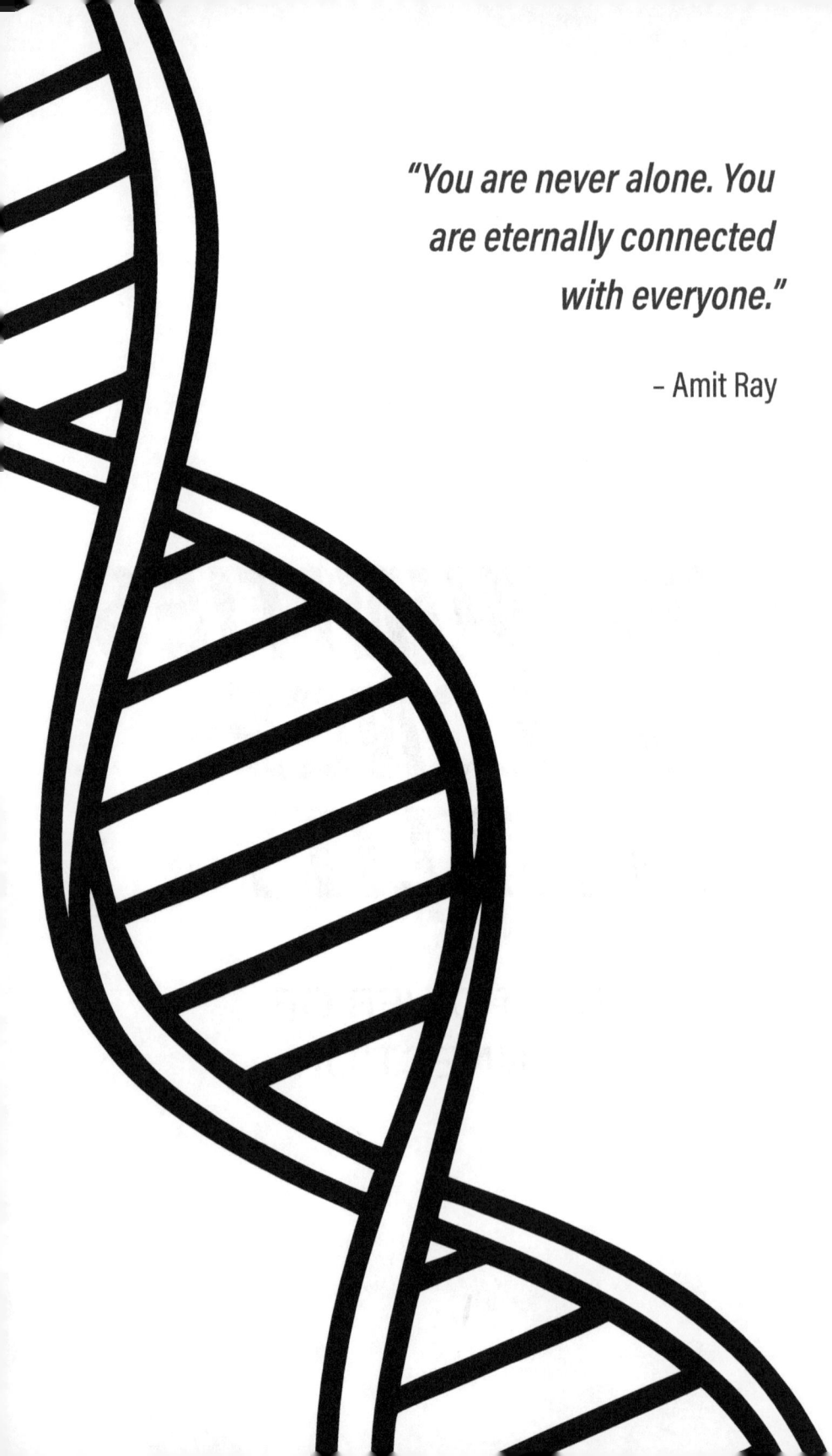

"You are never alone. You are eternally connected with everyone."

– Amit Ray

AN OFTEN-OVERLOOKED ELEMENT OF LONGE-VITALITY

When we think about the foundations of a long, vital life, our minds tend to gravitate to the usual suspects: nutrition, movement, restorative sleep, and stress mastery. But both emerging science and ancient wisdom remind us of another force, equally potent, often overlooked: the profound power of human connection.

We're born into relationships. From our first breath, our survival depends on others. This isn't just sentiment; it's biology. Humans are wired for connection through neural pathways, hormonal cascades, and immune responses that respond to social bonds like a key to a lock. Strong relationships can improve cardiovascular health and immune function.[1] In contrast, loneliness isn't just unpleasant – it's toxic. A landmark meta-analysis found that chronic social isolation increases the risk of premature death by 26 percent, while other research equates its health toll to smoking 15 cigarettes a day.[2]

If you need living proof, look to the world's 'longevity hotspots' – the Blue Zones. As mentioned in chapter three, in Okinawa, Japan, elders form *moais*, lifelong circles of friends who provide emotional, social, and even financial support. In the highlands of Sardinia, multigenerational households keep elders not in retirement, but in the heart of daily life. In Nicoya, Costa Rica, neighbours drop by unannounced for coffee, connection, and laughter. Across these diverse cultures, community isn't an accessory to health; it's the backbone.

Even in my own life, I've seen how connection fuels vitality. My grandmothers, FC Wong and SL Wong, lived in communities where no celebration was too small to share, and no hardship was borne alone. Their social fabric was woven from the threads of shared meals, festivals, and mutual care.

In this chapter, we'll explore the science of connection and the stories of those who live it. You'll see how a shared laugh can lower your cortisol levels, how belonging can buffer life's storms, and how connection – be it in a village, a running club, or a family kitchen – may just be the most powerful longevity medicine available.

THE *MOAI* OF OKINAWA: LIFELONG SOCIAL SUPPORT

Moai, loosely translated, means "meeting for a common purpose," but a *moai* is more than a social club – it's a covenant of care. Formed in childhood or early adulthood, members pledge to stand by each other for life.[3] These aren't casual acquaintances; they're chosen kin, bound by trust, reciprocity, and shared history.

Walk through an Okinawan village, and you might see an elderly group, silver hair glinting in the sun, gathered under a banyan tree. They laugh over cups of green tea, swap news about grandchildren, play hanafuda card games, and keep a watchful eye on one another. If someone is unwell, the *moai* organises meals, visits, or even financial assistance. In times of celebration, the joy is multiplied; in times of grief, the sorrow is halved.

As mentioned, Okinawa boasts one of the world's highest concentrations of centenarians, many of them women who maintain vitality, mobility, and sharp minds well into their 90s and beyond. Research consistently shows that social integration reduces the risk of mortality, cardiovascular disease, and cognitive decline.[4] In essence, close relationships are the single most important predictor of health and happiness in later life.[5]

In Okinawa, these protective relationships aren't left to chance; they're cultivated intentionally over decades. This is what sets the *moai* apart from typical Western friendships, which may dissolve with changes in job, geography, or life stage. The *moai* is a lifelong anchor, creating a social safety net that buffers stress and promotes resilience at a biological level.

While diet, physical activity, and genetics all play their part, Okinawan longevity is inseparable from this culture of enduring connection. Their lives are stitched together with the golden thread of belonging – a thread strong enough to hold them steady through life's storms. Through *moai,* the

Okinawans teach us a vital lesson: in the pursuit of a long, healthy life, the company you keep may be as important as the food you eat or the miles you run.

GRACE JONES:
A BRITISH BEACON OF CONNECTION

In 2018, Grace Jones of Worcestershire, UK, celebrated her 112th birthday, making her the oldest living person in Britain at the time. Her secret to longevity? Grace's daughter described her as "very lively and interested in everything and everyone."[6] Essentially, she enjoyed connecting with people.

Grace's life was a testament to the sustaining power of social bonds. She never withdrew from the rhythms that had anchored her for decades, maintaining friendships across generations. Even in her later years, when her mobility waned, Grace remained socially mobile – her world still filled with conversation, laughter, and care.

From Okinawa's *moai* to the Sardinian village squares where elders gather daily, longevity hotspots share a common thread: embeddedness in community life. In these environments, social connection isn't scheduled; it's woven into the fabric of everyday living. Meals are shared, milestones are celebrated collectively, and no one is left to face hardship alone.

Biologically, connection protects us. Positive social ties

lower cortisol levels and inflammation, which slows cellular wear and tear, and promote cardiovascular health and immune function.[7] Mentally, being part of a community keeps cognitive pathways active through conversation, storytelling, and problem-solving, protecting against neurodegenerative diseases such as dementia.[8]

Grace Jones' quiet wisdom around maintaining social connections is more than a quaint sentiment. It's a prescription for life. In a world where disconnection is increasingly common, her story invites us to re-prioritise relationships as essential daily nourishment, not an optional extra. For those seeking *Longe-Vitality*, connection is key.

MY GRANDMOTHERS: THE VILLAGE WISDOM OF CONNECTION

Neither of my grandmothers had ever heard of Okinawa or the Blue Zones, but they embodied the same principles that researchers now recognise as pillars of healthy ageing.

SL Wong was a quiet matriarch in a suburban low-rise without lifts, rising before dawn to deliver herbal remedies and hot meals to neighbours. FC Wong ran a bustling household where the kettle was always on and the door always open. In their worlds, community wasn't an optional extra; it was the fabric of life. They shared meals with neighbours, celebrated weddings and mourned deaths side by side, taught children the values of kindness and responsibility, and offered guidance to the next generation. Even as their physical strength waned, their social strength remained. Their counsel was still sought, their stories still told. They remained needed, valued, and deeply connected.

Modern science affirms what my grandmothers lived intuitively: strong social bonds protect not only our hearts but our very cells. According to research, people with robust social relationships have a 50 percent greater likelihood of survival over time compared to those with weaker ties – an effect comparable to quitting smoking.[9] Harvard Study of Adult Development has shown that strong social bonds are a better predictor of healthy ageing than cholesterol levels or blood pressure.[10] Connection also protects the brain. Older adults with rich social networks have slower rates of cognitive decline and lower incidence of dementia.[11] The mechanisms are manifold: shared laughter reduces stress hormones; empathy boosts oxytocin, and the emotional security of belonging helps regulate inflammation and cardiovascular health. Overall, close relationships are one of the strongest predictors of happiness and longevity, outweighing wealth, fame, and even baseline medical status.[12]

Connection operates as both shield and tonic. It buffers the physiological toll of stress, helps regulate inflammation, and fosters a sense of meaning and belonging – factors increasingly recognised as biological necessities, not luxuries. This aligns with findings from Blue Zone communities, where elders remain socially embedded, contributing to communal life well into their 90s and 100s.

When I think of my grandmothers, I see more than two remarkable women. I see living proof that feeling that you matter to others – being woven into a fabric of care and reciprocity – is perhaps one of the most potent medicines for *Longe-Vitality*. Their legacy is a reminder: we don't age well in isolation. We age well in the company of others, in circles where our presence continues to have purpose.

THE SCIENCE OF SOCIAL CONNECTION

When researchers began mapping the habits of the world's longest-lived people, they expected to find vegetables, exercise, and good sleep. What surprised them was how often another factor appeared – not in the form of food or fitness, but friendship. Whether it's the *moais* of Okinawa, the tight-knit fishing crews of Ikaria, or the morning market chatter of Sardinia, deep social bonds are a common thread running through longevity hotspots.

The last decade has brought a surge of research confirming what these cultures have always known: connection isn't just pleasant; it's protective. A 2023 meta-analysis found that people with poor social relationships face a 33 percent higher risk of early death.[13] The implications are clear: isolation isn't just a social problem; it's also a biological one.

Cardiovascular health appears to be one of the biggest beneficiaries of belonging. Research shows that richer social networks lower the risk of cardiovascular events, including coronary heart disease, heart failure, and stroke.[14] Our arteries, it seems, respond not just to diet and exercise, but also to dinner invitations and shared laughter.

The benefits extend to the brain. Longitudinal research from the University of New South Wales found that older adults who engage in regular, meaningful social interaction have a significantly reduced risk of developing dementia.[15] Conversation, storytelling, and even gentle disagreement stimulate neural circuits in ways solitary activity can't, helping preserve cognitive function deep into later life.

Even our stress systems respond to human warmth. Research demonstrates that people with strong social bonds have lower cortisol levels – the hormone that surges during stress.[16] In a lonely body, stress lingers like smoke after a fire. In a connected body, it clears more quickly, leaving room for restoration.

Essentially, relationships act as a psychological buffer, shielding us from anxiety, depression, and the slow erosion of wellbeing that can come from isolation. In *Longe-Vitality* terms, social connection is as non-negotiable as daily movement or a nutritious diet. In the end, it may be the company we keep – not just the calories we count – that most determines how well, and how long, we live.

CONNECTION IS MEDICINE

In many ancient cultures, healing was never confined to a single place or a single profession. It wasn't limited to sterile hospital wards or the domain of the physician's prescription pad. It was woven into the rhythm of everyday life – in kitchens where families gathered to prepare food together, in the glow of fire pits where stories were shared under the stars, in the gentle cadence of footsteps during daily walks, and in the circles where elders passed down wisdom as naturally as breathing. Healing was, at its core, a communal act. The individual thrived because the group thrived. A neighbour's wellbeing affected your own because you saw, heard, and touched each other's lives every day.

Fast-forward to today, and we find ourselves living in an era of unprecedented digital connection, yet physical, emotional, and social disconnection is widespread. We scroll through hundreds of updates on our phones but often struggle to recall the last time we had a deep, unhurried conversation in person. Loneliness is now recognised as a public health crisis, quietly eroding our physical vitality and mental resilience.

The solution is deceptively simple, but in our fast-paced, individualistic world, it requires conscious effort. We must reclaim the village and rebuild the small, everyday bonds that sustain us. It doesn't have to mean grand gestures or dramatic lifestyle overhauls. Sometimes the medicine is a slow walk with a neighbour at sunset, the shared comfort of preparing a meal with friends, or the warmth of calling a sibling just to hear their voice.

It might be rediscovering the camaraderie of your local running group, where shared miles turn into shared stories and the act of moving side by side naturally invites conversation that might never happen across a cafe table. It could be joining a choir, where breathing in harmony fosters something deeper than music, or tending a community garden, where hands in the soil turn strangers into teammates.

These micro-moments of connection aren't trivial. They're transformational. They recalibrate our nervous systems, soften the edges of stress, and remind us that we're part of something bigger than ourselves. The science of longevity shows us that meaningful relationships are as potent a predictor of healthspan as diet and exercise, but even without the data, our bodies and hearts already know the truth. We *feel* it.

CONNECTION IN MOTION – THE RUN DOC COMMUNITY

Through my coaching work and clinical care, I've witnessed how people light up when they belong. I've seen exhausted runners finish a race not because they felt strong, but because a friend's cheer carried them forward. I founded the Run Doc community with this in mind – not simply to help people run faster or train smarter, but to help them feel less alone in the journey.

When we lace up together, we aren't just logging kilometres. We're exchanging energy, encouragement, and quiet companionship. Connection isn't an optional extra in the pursuit of *Longe-Vitality*. It's the medicine we were designed to take daily.

RUN DOC'S LONGE-VITALITY TIPS

1

Join a tribe.
Whether it's a running crew, walking group, book club, or faith community, immerse yourself in groups that align with your values.

2

Schedule connection.
Just as you would a doctor's appointment, schedule time for relationships. Coffee with a friend. Weekly calls. Sunday lunches.

3

Be the connector.
Don't wait for community to find you. Invite others. Host dinners. Start a group chat. Build the network you want to live in.

4

Volunteer or mentor.
Purpose grows when we give. Share your time, knowledge, or kindness. It nourishes others and returns to you tenfold.

5

Walk and talk.
Combine movement with connection. A simple walk with a friend hits multiple longevity levers at once: exercise, fresh air, and emotional uplift.

TOGETHER, WE THRIVE

The truth is ancient, but we forget it in our rush: we're not meant to live in isolation. Our biology, our brains, and our spirits are designed to connect. To share life. To carry one another. To celebrate and mourn and laugh in community.

Longe-Vitality isn't just about surviving to 120.
It's about flourishing there: with a hand to
hold, a story to share, and people
who are glad you're alive.

So the next time you lace up your shoes or sit down for a meal, ask yourself: Who can I share this with? Because the road to a long, vital life is rarely walked alone. And that's exactly the point.

CHAPTER 11

THE LEGACY OF LONGE-VITALITY

LIVING AND LEAVING WELL

"Existence transcends mere chronological progression; it's about imbuing each moment with purpose and optimising the human experience."

– The Run Doc

THE FINAL LAP: LEAVING A LEGACY BEYOND LONGEVITY

This book has never been about chasing longevity as an end in itself. It has been about the art and science of living fully – about stacking joy, vitality, and connection so generously into your days that the years simply have no choice but to expand. Yes, we've spoken about extending life, but only through the deeper lens of enhancing life's quality, depth, and meaning.

Now, as we enter this final chapter, the conversation widens. It's no longer just about your endurance, your resilience, your joy in movement. It's about the ripples your life creates, the influence that continues beyond your own race clock. This is where *Longe-Vitality* evolves into legacy – what you stand for, what you give, and how you inspire others long after your own footsteps fade.

A legacy isn't built in grand gestures alone. It's forged in the everyday choices: offering kindness when it's inconvenient, showing up when it's easier to stay home, lacing your shoes even when your body protests. It's in the stories you tell, the habits you model, the encouragement you give to someone who's just starting their journey.

You don't need to be an Olympian or a world record holder to leave an enduring mark. The most powerful legacies are often left by the quiet, consistent, everyday heroes – the octogenarian who still joins the parkrun, the neighbour who tends the community garden, the parent who teaches their children that movement is joy, not punishment.

Living well into your later years isn't the end of the story. It's the bridge to what you leave behind. Your endurance, your laughter, your wisdom, your example – they become part of someone else's starting line.

In the end, the legacy of *Longe-Vitality* isn't measured in finish times, but in the number of people you've helped start their race.

JOHN WOODEN: TEACHING UNTIL THE FINAL BUZZER

Legendary basketball coach John Wooden once said, "Success is peace of mind, which is a direct result of self-satisfaction in knowing you did your best to become the best that you are capable of becoming." John didn't just preach this to college athletes chasing championships. He embodied it, day after day, decade after decade, until the final whistle of his own remarkable life.

Into his 90s, he still saw himself as a teacher. Not just of sport, but of values: discipline, humility, integrity, and consistency. His 'Pyramid of Success' wasn't a playbook for basketball; it was a blueprint for living. Even in his later years, when many slow down, John's calendar remained full.

He held weekly seminars, wrote reflective books, answered handwritten letters from former players, and mentored young coaches who sought his wisdom. His office may have been smaller than the arena he once commanded, but its influence reached far wider.

For John, the real measure of a life wasn't the trophies gathering dust on a shelf, but the character imprinted on the people he'd touched. That's why his former players spoke less about his game strategy and more about his kindness, moral courage, and quiet consistency. He showed that true leadership outlives the scoreboard.

In many ways, John's example mirrors the principle of *Longe-Vitality*. A long, vital life isn't just about maintaining your own healthspan; it's about using your added years as an amplifier for good. You can't take your medals with you, but you can leave behind a ripple of influence that shapes others long after you're gone.

Research in gerontology backs this up: purpose and contribution are as vital to longevity as nutrition or exercise. A 2013 study showed that volunteering regularly is associated with a reduced risk of mortality, even after adjusting for other health-related behaviours.[1]

John Wooden was a living embodiment of this science. His post-coaching decades were rich with purpose, community, and contribution. Like a seasoned ultrarunner pacing a newcomer through their first finish line, he saw his role as guiding others further than they believed they could go. And that's the heartbeat of a legacy: lifting others, not just for a moment, but for a lifetime.

In endurance sport, we sometimes talk about 'negative splits' – running the second half of a race faster than the first. John ran a life of negative splits. His later years weren't a slow fade but an acceleration into deeper impact. For those of us seeking *Longe-Vitality*, this offers a profound challenge: What if the years after our so-called 'prime' could be our most powerful, our most giving, our most meaningful?

Living well and leaving well are inseparable. You can't wait until the end to craft a legacy; it's woven into the small, daily choices – showing up, being consistent, choosing principle over convenience, offering encouragement when it's least expected. As John proved, the true final buzzer isn't the day you stop working; it's the day you stop making a difference.

MY GRANDMOTHERS: ORDINARY ACTS OF EXTRAORDINARY LONGEVITY

Closer to home, I look to my own grandmothers. While they left no monuments behind, they left something greater: a legacy of love expressed through action. In the kitchen, in the garden, in the market, they modelled how to live and leave well. Their legacy wasn't measured in wealth or possessions, but in the countless lives they nourished.

As I lace up my shoes each morning – whether for a 5 am long run or a slow recovery jog – I carry their example. In every step I take as a doctor, a runner, a coach, I hear their footsteps behind me, steady and sure. They remind me that life is a gift to be walked out in service and the true legacy of longevity isn't just how long we live, but how deeply we love and how fully we contribute.

While the science of *Longe-Vitality* can be summarised in graphs, hazard ratios, and p-values, its truest proof lies in lives like theirs. Ordinary women. Extraordinary lives. And in the quiet echo of their footsteps, I'm reminded that the finish line isn't the end. It's the legacy we leave in others, and the love we carry forward in each mile.

LEGACY IS LIVED NOW, NOT LATER

We often imagine legacy as something we leave after we're gone: a will, a building with our name, a fund in our honour. But the truth is, legacy is written in the present tense. It's in the footprints we leave today – in every conversation, every gesture, every stride.

For me, legacy is as much about how I lace up my shoes as it is about the finish lines I cross. It's the choice to go for that sunrise run even when my body whispers, "Stay in bed," demonstrating to my children, friends, and patients what persistence looks like. It's the way I share my recovery tips with a newer runner, or cook a meal packed with nourishing whole foods for my family after a long day.

Legacy is the living proof of your values,
played out in thousands of small acts.

Research reminds us that the ripple effects of our lifestyle extend far beyond our own health. The Framingham Heart Study – now spanning three generations – shows that healthy behaviours modelled by one person significantly increase the likelihood that close friends and relatives will adopt similar habits.[2]

Your legacy isn't just measured in years lived; it's measured in lives touched. Every time you invite a colleague to join you for a lunchtime walk instead of a sit-down meeting, or help a neighbour plant a garden, you're investing in someone else's health and vitality. These are the invisible chapters of your story, written in the bodies, minds, and spirits of others.

In the end, living and leaving well means choosing to be an example worth following. Not perfect, just consistent, generous, and present. Legacy isn't a future event. It's your daily training plan for life.

THE SCIENCE OF LEGACY AND LONGEVITY

From a biological perspective, the seeds of legacy begin in our DNA, but they're nurtured in our daily habits. We know from epigenetic research that lifestyle choices – the foods we eat, the miles we log, the sleep we protect – can switch genes on or off, influencing not just our own health but potentially that of future generations. This is legacy at the cellular level: our grandchildren's mitochondria may one day thank us for every salad, sunrise run, and night we turned in early. On the social side, legacy is the transmission of values, traditions, and behaviours that promote health and vitality.

The science of legacy also includes behavioural contagion. Studies show that physically active individuals often inspire peers to adopt similar habits, with measurable increases in physical activity levels among their social networks.[3] Every time you lace up, you're not just training your heart; you're quietly giving others permission to believe they can too.

The real finish line isn't 42.195 kilometres. It's knowing your life's race has left the course better for those still running it. A personal best fades; a personal legacy lasts. By training for life, not just for the next event, we create a dual legacy – one written in the strength of our own bodies and the vitality of those we influence.

When we live this way, our obituary becomes less about what we did and more about who we were. We leave behind fitter families, stronger communities, and maybe – just maybe – a world where the next generation sees health not as a chore, but as a joyful, lifelong pursuit. That, to me, is the ultimate *Longe-Vitality* legacy: living well, so others can too.

COACHING WITH LEGACY IN MIND

In my own work, I've coached young athletes chasing their first finish line, recovering patients reclaiming their independence, and seniors rediscovering the joy of movement after decades of sedentary living. Across these diverse journeys, the common denominator in those who truly thrive isn't raw speed or brute strength – it's meaning.

I see coaching as planting trees under whose shade we may never sit. Sometimes the 'win' isn't a personal best time, but watching someone you've guided run their first kilometre without stopping, or seeing someone once hesitant to move beam with the pride of crossing a finish line. These moments ripple outward, affecting families, communities, and future generations.

Living and leaving well is about aligning our movement with our values. It's about choosing to run not just for our own healthspan, but to inspire others to move towards theirs. The science tells us that purpose adds years to life and life to years. The stories remind us that purpose turns those years into a legacy worth leaving.

Because when the miles are done, and the shoes are hung up, what remains isn't how fast we went, but how deeply we moved – both ourselves and those who followed in our footsteps.

EVERY ACTION IS AN INHERITANCE

What will your great-grandchildren remember of you? That you ran a sub-3 marathon? Maybe. That you hiked mountains or completed a triathlon? Perhaps. But more often than not, they'll recall the quiet moments: how you smiled while tying your shoes, the way you got up day after day with grit and joy, how you treated others with kindness and respect.

Legacy is built in the rhythms of daily life. It's in the small, repeated actions that define a person long before accolades or statistics. The morning stretch, the walk to the market, the bike ride around the neighbourhood, or the deliberate pause to listen to a friend – these are the moments that accumulate into a life worth remembering.

Consider your rituals as deposits into the future. Every time you choose movement over inertia, patience over frustration, empathy over indifference, you're shaping the story others will tell. Your great-grandchildren may not remember the exact distance you ran or the PR you set, but they will carry forward the lessons embedded in your consistency, your resilience, and your capacity to show up.

Legacy is also in the narratives we weave. The stories you tell, the humour you share, the wisdom you pass along – these are the invisible threads that connect generations. Your life becomes a living archive, and every interaction, every small habit, becomes part of that archive.

In this sense, *Longe-Vitality* isn't only about the years you add to life but the life you infuse into each year. It's about living well so those who follow can learn not only how to survive, but how to thrive. It's about showing up fully in each moment, with intention and presence, so your energy, values, and joy echo beyond your own time.

As I remind my patients, endurance isn't just measured in miles or minutes, but in consistency, purpose, and heart. The legacy of *Longe-Vitality* isn't a trophy on a shelf; it's the imprint you leave in the hearts, habits, and stories of those who follow. Every step, every choice, every act of care and courage becomes an inheritance – a gift that outlives you, shaping the lives of generations yet to come.

RUN DOC'S FIVE LEGACY-BUILDING PRINCIPLES

1 **Define your purpose.**
Ask: *What gets me up in the morning? What legacy am I building in this moment?*

2 **Move daily.**
Whether it's walking, yoga, or active play with your kids, movement is the ink with which you write your story.

3 **Mentor and model.**
Teach, share, and coach, not by preaching, but by example. Your actions speak louder than advice.

4 **Celebrate simplicity.**
Legacy doesn't require epic feats. Folding laundry with presence, listening without distraction, showing up for a friend – these matter.

5 **Plan your exit with grace.**
Legacy includes how we leave, not just how we live. Reflect on the values you want to be remembered for, and live them now.

YOUR LEGACY BEINGS NOW

The journey of *Longe-Vitality* isn't linear; it spirals outward. From your cells to your soul. From your footsteps to someone else's inspiration. From movement to memory.

You may be at the start of your journey. Or you may be in your final lap. Either way, the question remains: *What are you passing on?* You've made it this far, so you already know the answer. It's not wealth. Not fame. Not medals. It's your way of being: moving with purpose, living with heart, and leaving behind a trail lit with vitality, *Longe-Vitality*.

Whether it's your first run or your thousandth, remember: with purpose and motion.

The Run Doc

Longe-Vitality isn't a destination; it's a journey, and your next mile starts now. To connect with me and learn about living a long and vital life, scan the QR code or follow the link.

Let's take this journey together.

@the_run_doc

ACKNOWLEDGEMENTS

Longe-Vitality has been a long run: one filled with unexpected hills, breathtaking vistas, and the steady support of people who have kept me going when the legs and spirit were tired. This book would not have been possible without those who have inspired, challenged, and believed in me from the very beginning. It is as much yours as it is mine.

To my father, Andy: thank you for always being there in your own quiet, steadfast way. You've been my cheer squad, my philosophical sounding board, and the guy who still laughs when I say I'm in the "top 2 percent of sons." Your dry humour and deep wisdom continue to guide me, and your unwavering support gave me the confidence to write this book not just as a doctor or runner, but as your son.

To Dr Ken, my running student turned fellow traveller on this *Longe-Vitality* journey: you've pushed the boundaries of what I thought possible, both on the track and in the world of medicine. Your cool competitive fire, combined with deep insight and friendship, has stretched me in all the best ways. You've proven that coaching is a two-way street, and I'm forever grateful for the miles we've logged and will continue to log together, physically and metaphorically.

To my life partner, Louise: my real-life Louise Sawyer in *Thelma and Louise.* If I'm the one writing the map, you're the one driving the getaway car with music blasting and laughter filling the air. You know exactly what to say and when to say it, lighting fires in my soul when needed and calming the storm when it brews. You've believed in *Longe-Vitality* even before I found the words for it. You are not just the *wind beneath my wings;* you are the sky I fly through, the fuel in my stride, and the reason this book carries heart as well as science.

A heartfelt thank you to Dale and Gilbert of the Sydney Striders Run Club. You both introduced me, and later my son Johann, to the beautiful world of running. Long before I became an Athletics Australia Level 3 Run Coach, you showed me what it means to lead, to pace, to guide. You taught me that running is not just an individual pursuit, but a gift we share, a discipline we pass down. Watching Johann grow under your mentorship is one of my greatest joys, and I continue to nurture and develop his talents to this day.

To my patients, my coaching clients, my running community: this book draws its wisdom and soul from you. Every consultation, every lap around the track, every race debrief has fed into the fabric of *Longe-Vitality.* You are the living proof that it is never too late to begin again, to move forward with purpose, and to shape your own definition of a long, vital life.

Finally, to the readers: whether you're lacing up for your first walk around the block or training for your tenth ultramarathon, thank you. Thank you for picking up this book, for trusting this journey, and for believing that your best years are not behind you, but ahead, pulsing with promise.

May this book inspire you to run long, live fully, and leave a legacy not just of years, but of meaning.

Longe-Vitality, the Run Doc way!

ABOUT THE AUTHOR

Dr Jenson Mak, widely known as 'The Run Doc', is a healthy ageing and longevity specialist who transformed his life and practice through the power of movement. Once nicknamed 'The Fat Doc', Jenson stood on the precipice of unhealth: battling high blood pressure, insomnia, work stress, and mental health challenges. But the turning point came when he realised that if he didn't make a change, he risked missing out on life's most precious moments, those shared with his three young children.

Determined to show up fully for his family, Jenson began running. What started as a desperate sprint toward better health evolved into a lifelong journey of purpose, vitality, and scientific discovery. He went on to become one of the first to achieve Level 3 Performance Development Coach accreditation with Athletics Australia, spanning road, trail, and ultra disciplines. He is also a certified Primal Health Coach, clinical researcher, senior lecturer in clinical medicine, and a

Justice of the Peace.

Blending science, soul, and stride, Jenson brings a unique perspective to the conversation around longevity. His lived experience, paired with insights from over 10,000 patients and many more coaching encounters, makes him a trusted voice in healthy ageing. Off the trails, he enjoys singing karaoke classics and diving deep into books on psychology, always chasing the harmony between mind, body, and meaning.

ENDNOTES

Chapter 1

1   The Nobel Prize (n.d.) 'Nobel Prize in Physiology or Medicine 2009', accessed 8 September 2025, https://www.nobelprize.org/prizes/medicine/2009/summary/.

2   Shammas MA (2011) 'Telomeres, Lifestyle, Cancer, and Aging', *Current Opinion in Clinical Nutrition and Metabolic Care*, 14(1):28–34, doi.org/10.1097/MCO.0b013e32834121b1.

3   Fisher MZ (29 September 2021) 'At 92 Years Young, the "Iron Nun" is Still Running', *Triathlete,* accessed 9 September 2025, https://www.triathlete.com/culture/people/at-91-years-young-the-iron-nun-is-still-running.

4   Kawaguchi J (2008) 'Dr Shigeaki Hinohara – Medical Doctor, Author, Composer | Words to Live by', *Judit Kawaguchi,* accessed 9 September 2025, https://judittokyo.com/words-to-live-by/dr-shigeaki-hinohara/;
Popomaronis T (26 August 2020) 'Japanese Doctor Who Lived to 105 – His Spartan diet, Views on Retirement, and Other Rare Longevity Tips', *CNBC,* accessed 9 September 2025, https://www.cnbc.com/2020/08/26/japanese-doctor-lived-to-105-spartan-diet-retirement-views-rare-longevity-tips.html.

5   Kawaguchi J (2008) 'Dr Shigeaki Hinohara – Medical Doctor, Author, Composer | Words to Live by', *Judit Kawaguchi,* accessed 9 September 2025, https://judittokyo.com/words-to-live-by/dr-shigeaki-hinohara/.

6   Albert V (22 February 2020) 'Tao Porchon-Lynch, Named World's Oldest Yoga Teacher, Has Died at 101', *CBS News,* accessed 9 September 2025, https://www.cbsnews.com/news/tao-porchon-lynch-worlds-oldest-yoga-teacher-has-died-at-101/.

7　Pangambam S (1 January 2021) 'There is Nothing You Cannot Do: Tao Porchon-Lynch (Transcript)', *The Singju Post,* accessed 9 September 2025, https://singjupost.com/there-is-nothing-you-cannot-do-tao-porchon-lynch-transcript/.

8　Yoga Teachers Association (31 March 2020) 'Reflections on Tao Porchon-Lynch by Renee Diamond', accessed 9 September 2025, https://www.ytayoga.com/YTAYogaBlog/9005637.

9　Reuters (29 November 2010) 'For Yoga Master at 92, There Is Only the Dance', *Reuters,* accessed 9 September 2025, https://www.reuters.com/article/lifestyle/for-yoga-master-at-92-there-is-only-the-dance-idUSTRE6AS1XO/.

10　Lohman T, Bains G, Cole S, Gharibvand LB, and Lohman E (2023) 'High-Intensity Interval Training Reduces Transcriptomic Age: A Randomized Controlled Trial', *Aging Cell,* 22(6), doi.org/10.1111/acel.13841.

11　Lohman T, Bains G, Cole S, Gharibvand LB, and Lohman E (2023) 'High-Intensity Interval Training Reduces Transcriptomic Age: A Randomized Controlled Trial', *Aging Cell,* 22(6), doi.org/10.1111/acel.13841.

12　Scripps Research Institute (n.d.) 'Healthy Aging – Wellderly', accessed 9 September 2025, https://www.scripps.edu/science-and-medicine/translational-institute/translational-research/genomic-medicine/wellderly/.

13　Kee C (27 May 2025) 'I'm a Cardiologist. Adding This 1 Exercise to My Routine Made Me Fitter Than Ever at 70', *Today,* accessed 9 September 2025, https://www.today.com/health/diet-fitness/cardiologist-tip-strenght-training-aging-rcna208034.

14　Topol E (2025) *Super Agers: An Evidence-Based Approach to Longevity,* Simon & Schuster.

15　Revelo Herrera SG and Leon-Rojas JE (2024) 'The Effect of Aerobic Exercise in Neuroplasticity, Learning, and Cognition: A Systematic Review', *Cureus,* 16(2):e54021, doi.org/10.7759/cureus.54021.

16 Kong L, Miu L, Yao W, and Shi Z (2024) 'Effect of Regular Aerobic Exercise on Cognitive Function, Depression Level and Regulative Role of Neurotrophic Factor: A Prospective Cohort Study in the Young and the Middle-Aged Sample', *Risk Management and Healthcare Policy*, 17:935–943, doi.org/10.2147/RMHP.S456765.

17 Godman H (3 April 2013) 'Which Is Better for Keeping Your Mind Fit: Physical or Mental Activity?', *Harvard Health Publishing*, accessed 15 September 2025, https://www.health.harvard.edu/blog/which-is-better-for-keeping-your-mind-fit-physical-or-mental-activity-201304036049.

18 Buettner D and Skemp S (2016) 'Blue Zones: Lessons from the World's Longest Lived', *American Journal of Lifestyle Medicine*, 10(5):318–321, doi.org/10.1177/1559827616637066;
Tanno K, Sakata K, Ohsawa M, Onoda T, Itai K, Yaegashi Y, Tamakoshi A, and JACC Study Group (2009) 'Associations of Ikigai as a Positive Psychological Factor with All-Cause Mortality and Cause-Specific Mortality Among Middle-Aged and Elderly Japanese People: Findings from the Japan Collaborative Cohort Study', *Journal of Psychosomatic Research*, 67(1):67–75, doi.org/10.1016/j.jpsychores.2008.10.018.

19 Sone T, Nakaya N, Ohmori K, Shimazu T, Higashiguchi M, Kakizaki M, Kikuchi N, Kuriyama S, and Tsuji I (2008) 'Sense of Life Worth Living (Ikigai) and Mortality in Japan: Ohsaki Study', *Psychosomatic Medicine*, 70(6):709–715, doi.org/10.1097/PSY.0b013e31817e7e64.

20 Buettner D and Skemp S (2016) 'Blue Zones: Lessons from the World's Longest Lived', *American Journal of Lifestyle Medicine*, 10(5):318–321, doi.org/10.1177/1559827616637066.

21 Schnohr P, O'Keefe JH, Marott JL, Lange P, and Jensen GB (2015) 'Dose of Jogging and Long-Term Mortality: The Copenhagen City Heart Study', *Journal of the American College of Cardiology*, 65(5):411–419, doi.org/10.1016/j.jacc.2014.11.023.

22 Paffenbarger RS, Hyde RT, Wing AL, Lee IM, Jung DL, and Kampert JB (1993) 'The Association of Changes in Physical-Activity Level and Other Lifestyle Characteristics with Mortality Among Men', *The

New England Journal of Medicine, 328(8):538–545, doi.org/10.1056/NEJM199302253280804.

23   Qiu Y, Fernández-García B, Lehmann HI, Li G, Kroemer G, López-Otín C, and Xiao J (2023) 'Exercise Sustains the Hallmarks of Health', *Journal of Sport and Health Science*, 12(1):8–35, doi.org/10.1016/j.jshs.2022.10.003.

Chapter 2

1   Paluch AE, Gabriel KP, Fulton JE, Lewis CE, Schreiner PJ, Sternfeld B, Sidney S, Siddique J, Whitaker KM, and Carnethon MR (2021) 'Steps per Day and All-Cause Mortality in Middle-aged Adults in the Coronary Artery Risk Development in Young Adults Study', *JAMA Network Open*, 4(9):e2124516, doi.org/10.1001/jamanetworkopen.2021.24516.

2   Wang X, Liu F, Li J, Yang X, Chen J, Cao J, Wu X, Lu X, Huang J, Li Y, Zhao L, Shen C, Hu D, Yu L, Liu X, Wu X, Wu S, and Gu D (2020) 'Tea Consumption and the Risk of Atherosclerotic Cardiovascular Disease and All-Cause Mortality: The China-PAR Project', *European Journal of Preventive Cardiology*, 27(18):1956–1963, doi.org/10.1177/2047487319894685; Mancini E, Beglinger C, Drewe J, Zanchi D, Lang UE, and Borgwardt S (2017) 'Green Tea Effects on Cognition, Mood and Human Brain Function: A Systematic Review', *Phytomedicine: International Journal of Phytotherapy and Phytopharmacology*, 34:26–37, doi.org/10.1016/j.phymed.2017.07.008.

3   Babenko N, Elayoubi J, Haley W, and Small B (2024) 'Social Engagement and Depressive Symptoms: Differential Effects in Older Adults with and Without Cancer', *Innovation in Aging*, 8:747, doi.org/10.1093/geroni/igae098.2431.

4   Piolatto M, Bianchi F, Rota M, Marengoni A, Akbaritabar A, and Squazzoni F (2022) 'The Effect of Social Relationships on Cognitive Decline in Older Adults: An Updated Systematic Review and Meta-Analysis of Longitudinal Cohort Studies', *BMC Public Health*, 22(278), doi.org/10.1186/s12889-022-12567-5.

5   Amin SM, Khedr MA, Tawfik AF, Malek MGN, and El-Ashry AM (2025) 'The Mediating and Moderating Role of Social Support on the Relationship Between Psychological Well-Being and Burdensomeness Among Elderly with Chronic Illness: Community Nursing Perspective', *BMC Nursing,* 24(156), doi.org/10.1186/s12912-025-02743-4.

6   O'Bryan SJ, Giuliano C, Woessner MN, Vogrin S, Smith C, Duque G, and Levinger I (2022) 'Progressive Resistance Training for Concomitant Increases in Muscle Strength and Bone Mineral Density in Older Adults: A Systematic Review and Meta-Analysis', *Sports Medicine,* 52(8):1939–1960, doi.org/10.1007/s40279-022-01675-2.

7   Alimujiang A, Wiensch A, Boss J, Fleischer NL, Mondul AM, McLean K, Mukherjee B, and Pierce CL (2019) 'Association Between Life Purpose and Mortality Among US Adults Older than 50 years', *JAMA Network Open,* 2(5):e194270, doi.org/10.1001/jamanetworkopen.2019.4270.

8   Zaninotto P and Steptoe A (2019) 'Association Between Subjective Well-Being and Living Longer Without Disability or Illness', *JAMA Network Open,* 2(7):e196870, doi.org/10.1001/jamanetworkopen.2019.6870.

9   Diebel M (13 May 2016) 'This Woman Is the Only Person Left Born in the 1800s', *USA Today,* accessed 17 September 2025, https://www.usatoday.com/story/news/world/2016/05/13/shes-only-person-left-born-1800s/84321322/.

10 SBS News (16 April 2017) 'Italian Emma Morano, Last Known Survivor of 19th Century, Dies at 117', accessed 17 September 2025, https://www.sbs.com.au/news/article/italian-emma-morano-last-known-survivor-of-19th-century-dies-at-117/97t769whj.

11 Di Donato V (29 November 2016) 'Oldest Living Person Credits Longevity to Raw Eggs, Independence', *CNN,* accessed 17 September 2025, https://edition.cnn.com/2016/11/29/health/oldest-living-person-emma-morano.

12 Willcox BJ, Willcox DC, Todoriki H, Fujiyoshi A, Yano K, He Q, Curb JD, and Suzuki M (2007) 'Caloric Restriction, the Traditional

Okinawan Diet, and Healthy Aging', *Annals of the New York Academy of Sciences*, 1114:434-455, doi.org/10.1196/annals.1396.037.

13 Musinguzi J (7 December 2022) 'Why Sarah Ntiro Remains a Woman of Her Own Pedigree', *The Observer,* accessed 17 September, https://observer.ug/news/why-sarah-ntiro-remains-a-woman-of-her-own-pedigree/.

14 World Health Organization (2020) 'Who Guidelines on Physical Activity and Sedentary Behaviour', accessed 17 September 2025, https://iris.who.int/bitstream/handle/10665/336656/9789240015128-eng.pdf.

15 Ekelund U et al. (2019) 'Dose-Response Associations Between Accelerometry Measured Physical Activity and Sedentary Time and All Cause Mortality: Systematic Review and Harmonised Meta-Analysis', *BMJ,* 336, doi.org/10.1136/bmj.l4570.

16 Mineo L (11 April 2011) 'Harvard Study, Almost 80 Years Old, Has Proved That Embracing Community Helps Us Live Longer, and Be Happier', *The Harvard Gazette,* accessed 17 September 2025, https://news.harvard.edu/gazette/story/2017/04/over-nearly-80-years-harvard-study-has-been-showing-how-to-live-a-healthy-and-happy-life/.

17 Shiba K, Kubzansky LD, Williams DR, VanderWeele TJ, and Kim ES (2022) 'Purpose in Life and 8-Year Mortality by Gender and Race/Ethnicity Among Older Adults in the U.S', *Preventive Medicine*, 164, doi.org/10.1016/j.ypmed.2022.107310.

18 Cherpak CE (2019) 'Mindful Eating: A Review of How the Stress-Digestion-Mindfulness Triad May Modulate and Improve Gastrointestinal and Digestive Function', *Integrative Medicine,* 18(4):48–53, https://pubmed.ncbi.nlm.nih.gov/32549835/.

19 Chen YC, Lee CS, Chiang MC, Tsui PL, Lan BK, and Chen YJ (2025) 'Nourishing Holistic Well-Being: The Role of Family Dynamics and Family Cooking', *Healthcare,* 13(4):414, doi.org/10.3390/healthcare13040414.

20 Lane M et al. (2024) 'Ultra-Processed Food Exposure and Adverse

Health Outcomes: Umbrella Review of Epidemiological Meta-Analyses', *BMJ*, 384, doi.org/10.1136/bmj-2023-077310.

Chapter 3

1   Herskind AM, McGue M, Holm NV, Sorenson TIA, Harvald B, and Vaupel JW (1996) 'The Heritability of Human Longevity: A Population-Based Study of 2872 Danish Twin Pairs Born 1870–1900', *Human Genetics,* 97:319–323, doi.org/10.1007/BF02185763.

2   Ruby JG et al. (2018) 'Estimates of the Heritability of Human Longevity Are Substantially Inflated Due to Assortative Mating', *Genetics*, 210(3):1109–1124, doi.org/10.1534/genetics.118.301613.

3   Timmers PRHJ et al. (2019) 'Genomics of 1 Million Parent Lifespans Implicates Novel Pathways and Common Diseases and Distinguishes Survival Chances', *eLife*, 8:e39856, doi.org/10.7554/eLife.39856.

4   Robine JM and Allard M (2003) 'Validation of Exceptional Longevity: Jeanne Calment: Validation of the Duration of Her Life', *Max Planck Institute,* accessed 18 September 2025, https://www.demogr. mpg.de/books/odense/6/09.htm.

5   Collins L (10 February 2020) 'Was Jeanne Calment the Oldest Person Who Ever Lived – or a Fraud?', *The New Yorker,* accessed 18 September 2025, https://www.newyorker.com/magazine/2020/02/17/was-jeanne-calment-the-oldest-person-who-ever-lived-or-a-fraud.

6   Whitney CR (5 August 1997) 'Jeanne Calment, World's Elder, Dies at 122', *New York Times,* accessed 18 September 2025, https://www. nytimes.com/1997/08/05/world/jeanne-calment-world-s-elder-dies-at-122.html; Steptoe A and Kivimäki M (2013) 'Stress and Cardiovascular Disease: An Update on Current Knowledge', *Annual Review of Public Health*, 34:337–354, doi.org/10.1146/annurev-publheal th-031912-114452.

7   Onque R (21 February 2023) 'The World's Oldest Person Made It to 122 – 3 Reasons She Lived So Long, from a Longevity Expert Who Knew Her', *CNBC,* accessed 18 September 2025, https://www.cnbc. com/2023/02/21/longevity-expert-3-reasons-the-worlds-oldest-per-

son-lived-to-122.html.

8 Ruby JG et al. (2018) 'Estimates of the Heritability of Human
   Longevity Are Substantially Inflated Due to Assortative Mating',
   Genetics, 210(3):1109–1124, doi.org/10.1534/genetics.118.301613;
   Herskind AM, McGue M, Holm NV, Sorenson TIA, Harvald B, and
   Vaupel JW (1996) 'The Heritability of Human Longevity: A Pop-
   ulation-Based Study of 2872 Danish Twin Pairs Born 1870–1900',
   Human Genetics, 97:319–323, doi.org/10.1007/BF02185763.

9 Holt-Lunstad J, Smith TB, and Layton JB (2010) 'Social Relationships and Mortality Risk: A Meta-Analytic Review', *PLoS Medicine*,
   7(7):e1000316, doi.org/10.1371/journal.pmed.1000316.

10 Steptoe A and Kivimäki M (2013) 'Stress and Cardiovascular Disease:
   An Update on Current Knowledge', *Annual Review of Public Health*,
   34:337–354, doi.org/10.1146/annurev-publhealth-031912-114452.

11 Buettner D (2016) 'Power 9: Reverse Engineering Longevity',
   Blue Zones, accessed 18 September 2025, https://www.bluezones.
   com/2016/11/power-9/.

12 Epel ES, Blackburn EH, Lin J, Dhabhar FS, Adler NE, Morrow JD,
   and Cawthon RM (2004) 'Accelerated Telomere Shortening in Response to Life Stress', *Proceedings of the National Academy of Sciences of
   the United States of America*, 101(49):17312–17315, doi.org/10.1073/
   pnas.0407162101.

13 Fraser GE (2009) 'Vegetarian Diets: What Do We Know of Their Effects on Common Chronic Diseases?', *The American Journal of Clinical
   Nutrition*, 89(5):1607S–1612S, doi.org/10.3945/ajcn.2009.26736K.

14 Di Castelnuovo A, Costanzo S, Bagnardi V, Donati MB, Iacoviello
   L, and de Gaetano G (2006) 'Alcohol Dosing and Total Mortality
   in Men and Women: An Updated Meta-Analysis of 34 Prospective
   Studies', *Archives of Internal Medicine*, 166(22):2437–2445, doi.
   org/10.1001/archinte.166.22.2437.

15 Buettner D (2016) 'Power 9: Reverse Engineering Longevity',
   Blue Zones, accessed 18 September 2025, https://www.bluezones.

com/2016/11/power-9/.

16   Lin Z, Yin X, Levy BR, Yuan Y, and Chen X (2024) 'Association of
     Family Support with Lower Modifiable Risk Factors for Dementia
     Among Cognitively Impaired Older Adults', *The American Jour-
     nal of Geriatric Psychiatry*, 32(10):1187–1199, doi.org/10.1016/j.
     jagp.2024.05.005.

17   Holt-Lunstad J, Smith TB, and Layton JB (2010) 'Social Relation-
     ships and Mortality Risk: A Meta-Analytic Review', *PLoS Medicine*,
     7(7):e1000316, doi.org/10.1371/journal.pmed.1000316.

18   Spira AP, Chen-Edinboro LP, Wu MN, and Yaffe K (2014) 'Im-
     pact of Sleep on the Risk of Cognitive Decline and Dementia',
     Current Opinion in Psychiatry, 27(6):478–483, doi.org/10.1097/
     YCO.0000000000000106.

19   Sabot D, Lovegrove R, and Stapleton P (2022) 'The Association
     Between Sleep Quality and Telomere Length: A Systematic Liter-
     ature Review', *Brain, Behavior, and Immunity – Health*, 28, doi.
     org/10.1016/j.bbih.2022.100577.

20   Du M, Liu M, and Liu J (2023) 'U-Shaped Association Between
     Sleep Duration and the Risk of Respiratory Diseases Mortality: A
     Large Prospective Cohort Study from UK Biobank', Journal of Clini-
     cal Sleep Medicine, 19(11):1923–1932, doi.org/10.5664/jcsm.10732.
     PMID: 37477156

21   Ornish D, Lin J, Daubenmier J, Weidner G, Epel E, Kemp C,
     Magbanua MJ, Marlin R, Yglecias L, Carroll PR, and Blackburn EH
     (2008) 'Increased Telomerase Activity and Comprehensive Life-
     style Changes: A Pilot Study', *The Lancet*, 9(11):1048–1057, doi.
     org/10.1016/S1470-2045(08)70234-1; Jirtle RL and Skinner MK
     (2007) 'Environmental Epigenomics and Disease Susceptibility', *Na-
     ture Reviews*, 8(4):253–262, doi.org/10.1038/nrg2045.

Chapter 4

1   Lee DH et al. (2022) 'Long-Term Leisure-Time Physical Activity

Intensity and All-Cause and Cause-Specific Mortality: A Prospective Cohort of US Adults', *Circulation,* 146(7), doi.org/10.1161/CIRCU-LATIONAHA.121.058162.

2   Ji H et al. (2024) 'Sex Differences in Association of Physical Activity with All-Cause and Cardiovascular Mortality', *JACC,* 83(8), doi.org/10.1016/j.jacc.2023.12.019.

3   Chettiar R (15 July 2025) 'Fauja Singh: Oldest Marathon Runner an Inspiration for Youngsters', *Olympics,* accessed 22 September 2025, https://www.olympics.com/en/news/who-is-fauja-singh-oldest-indi-an-origin-british-marathon-runner.

4   ET Online (17 July 2025) '"I Eat What I Grow": How World's Oldest Marathon Runner Fauja Singh's Punjabi Diet Powered 9 Marathons', *The Economic Times,* accessed 22 September 2025, https://economic-times.indiatimes.com/news/new-updates/i-eat-what-i-grow-how-worlds-oldest-marathon-runner-fauja-singhs-punjabi-diet-powered-9-marathons/articleshow/122591717.cms.

5   Chettiar R (15 July 2025) 'Fauja Singh: Oldest Marathon Runner an Inspiration for Youngsters', *Olympics,* accessed 22 September 2025, https://www.olympics.com/en/news/who-is-fauja-singh-oldest-indi-an-origin-british-marathon-runner.

6   Neiyyar D (20 April 2012) 'Oldest Marathon Runner Announced Retirement', *BBC,* accessed 22 September 2025, https://www.bbc.com/news/uk-england-london-17784505.

7   Park A (3 November 2023) 'The Deeper Story Behind Netflix's *Nyad*', *Time,* accessed 23 September 2025, https://time.com/6330894/nyad-movie-true-story-netflix/.

8   Park A (3 November 2023) 'The Deeper Story Behind Netflix's *Nyad*', *Time,* accessed 23 September 2025, https://time.com/6330894/nyad-movie-true-story-netflix/.

9   Mackenzie NG (19 July 2011) 'Diana Nyad's Insane Training Schedule', *ESPN,* accessed 23 September 2025, https://www.espn.com/espnw/features/article/6783753/diana-nyad-insane-training-schedule.

10 Pearce M (2 September 2013) 'Diana Nyad, After Swim: "You're Never Too Old to Chase Your Dreams', *Los Angeles Times,* accessed 23 September 2025, https://www.latimes.com/nation/nationnow/la-na-nn-diana-nyad-cuba-florida-remarks-20130902-story.html.

11 Joyner MJ and Coyle EF (2008) 'Endurance Exercise Performance: The Physiology of Champions', *The Journal of Physiology,* 586(1):34–44, doi.org/10.1113/jphysiol.2007.143834.

12 Nemoto K, Gen-no H, Masuki S, Okazaki K, and Nose H (2007) 'Effects of High-Intensity Interval Walking Training on Physical Fitness and Blood Pressure in Middle-Aged and Older People', *Mayo Clinic Proceedings*, 82(7):803–11, doi.org/10.4065/82.7.803. PMID: 17605959.

13 Garber C et al. (2011) 'Quantity and Quality of Exercise for Developing and Maintaining Cardiorespiratory, Musculoskeletal, and Neuromotor Fitness in Apparently Healthy Adults: Guidance for Prescribing Exercise', *Medicine & Science in Sports & Exercise,* 43(7):1334–1359, doi.org/10.1249/MSS.0b013e318213fefb.

14 Ungvari Z, Fazekas-Pongor V, Csiszar A, and Kunutsor SK (2023) 'The Multifaceted Benefits of Walking for Healthy Aging: From Blue Zones to Molecular Mechanisms', *GeroScience*. 45(6):3211–3239, doi.org/10.1007/s11357-023-00873-8.

15 Peterson MD, Rhea MR, Sen A, and Gordon PM (2010) 'Resistance Exercise for Muscular Strength in Older Adults: A Meta-Analysis,' *Ageing Research Reviews*, 9(3):226–237, doi.org/10.1016/j.arr.2010.03.004.

16 Cornelissen VA and Smart NA (2013) 'Exercise Training for Blood Pressure: A Systematic Review and Meta-Analysis', *Journal of the American Heart Association,* 2(1), doi.org/10.1161/JAHA.112.00447.

17 Zahalka SJ, Abushamat LA, Scalzo RL, and Reusch JEB (2025) 'The Role of Exercise in Diabetes', *Endotext,* https://www.ncbi.nlm.nih.gov/books/NBK549946/.

18 Mann S, Beedie C, and Jimenez A (2014) 'Differential Effects of

Aerobic Exercise, Resistance Training and Combined Exercise Modalities on Cholesterol and the Lipid Profile: Review, Synthesis and Recommendations', *Sports Medicine*, 44(2):211–21, doi.org/10.1007/s40279-013-0110-5.

19   Westcott WL (2012) 'Resistance Training Is Medicine: Effects of Strength Training on Health', *Current Sports Medicine Reports*, 11(4):209–216, doi.org/10.1249/JSR.0b013e31825dabb8. PMID: 22777332.

20   Sherrington C et al. (2017) 'Exercise to Prevent Falls in Older Adults: An Updated Systematic Review and Meta-Analysis', *British Journal of Sports Medicine*, 51:1750–1758, https://bjsm.bmj.com/content/51/24/1750.

21   Zhang J, Tam WWS, Hounsri K, Kusuyama J, and Wu VX (2024) 'Effectiveness of Combined Aerobic and Resistance Exercise on Cognition, Metabolic Health, Physical Function, and Health-Related Quality of Life in Middle-aged and Older Adults with Type 2 Diabetes Mellitus: A Systematic Review and Meta-Analysis', *Archives of Physical Medicine and Rehabilitation*, 105(8):1585-1599, https://doi.org/10.1016/j.apmr.2023.10.005.

Chapter 5

1   Eijsvogels TMH, Molossi S, Lee D, Emery MS, and Thompson PD (2016) 'Exercise at the Extremes: The Amount of Exercise to Reduce Cardiovascular Events', *Journal of the American College of Cardiology*, 67(3):316–329, https://doi.org/10.1016/j.jacc.2015.11.034; An J, Su Z, and Meng S (2024) 'Effect of Aerobic Training Versus Resistance Training for Improving Cardiorespiratory Fitness and Body Composition in Middle-Aged to Older Adults: A Systematic Review and Meta-Analysis of Randomized Controlled Trials', *Archives of Gerontology and Geriatrics*, 126, doi.org/10.1016/j.archger.2024.105530.

2   Ringholm S et al. (2023) 'Impact of Aging and Lifelong Exercise Training on Mitochondrial Function and Network Connectivity in Human Skeletal Muscle', *The Journals of Gerontology*, 78,(3):373–383, doi.org/10.1093/gerona/glac164.

3   Yan Z, Lira VA, and Greene NP (2012) 'Exercise Training-Induced Regulation of Mitochondrial Quality', *Exercise and Sport Sciences Reviews*, 40(3):159–164, doi.org/10.1097/JES.0b013e3182575599. PMID: 22732425; PMCID: PMC3384482.

4   Shepherd E (19 March 2018) 'Meet the 81-Year-Old Woman Who Can Bench Press 115lb', *BBC,* accessed 23 September 2025, https://www.bbc.com/bbcthree/article/bb27dc63-acda-4bb8-981f-988866ace2fd.

5   Gripped (2 May 2016) 'Carlos Soria Climbs Annapurna at 77 Years Old and Sets Record', *Gripped Magazine,* accessed 23 September 2025, https://gripped.com/routes/carlos-soria-climbs-annapurna-at-77-years-old-and-sets-record/.

6   Reuters (18 May 2023) 'Spanish Mountaineer, 84, Injured Just Short of Being Oldest to Scale World's 14 Highest Peaks', *Reuters,* accessed 23 September 2025, https://www.reuters.com/world/spanish-mountaineer-84-injured-just-short-goal-become-worlds-oldest-climber-2023-05-17/.

7   Stewart J (9 March 2013) 'The Pursuits Interview: Carlos Soria', *Financial Times,* accessed 23 September 2025, https://www.ft.com/content/4bd2bb14-85f8-11e2-9ee3-00144feabdc0.

8   Erickson KI et al. (2011) 'Exercise Training Increases Size of Hippocampus and Improves Memory', *PNAS*, 108(7): 3017–3022, doi.org/10.1073/pnas.1015950108.

9   Blondell SJ, Hammersley-Mather R, and Veerman JL (2014) 'Does Physical Activity Prevent Cognitive Decline and Dementia?: A Systematic Review and Meta-Analysis of Longitudinal Studies', *BMC Public Health,* 14(510), doi.org/10.1186/1471-2458-14-510.

10 Singh B et al. (2023) 'Effectiveness of Physical Activity Interventions for Improving Depression, Anxiety and Distress: An Overview of Systematic Reviews', *British Journal of Sports Medicine,* 57(18):1203–1209, doi.org/10.1136/bjsports-2022-106195.

11 Nieman DC and Wentz LM (2019) 'The Compelling Link Between

Physical Activity and the Body's Defense System', *Journal of Sport and Health Science*, 8(3):201–217, doi.org/10.1016/j.jshs.2018.09.009.

12 Shah SZA, Karam JA, Zeb A, Ullah R, Shah A, Haq IU, Ali I, Darain H, and Chen H (2021) 'Movement Is Improvement: The Therapeutic Effects of Exercise and General Physical Activity on Glycemic Control in Patients with Type 2 Diabetes Mellitus: A Systematic Review and Meta-Analysis of Randomized Controlled Trials', *Diabetes Therapy*, 12(3):707–732, doi.org/10.1007/s13300-021-01005-1.

13 Khera AV et al. (2016) 'Genetic Risk, Adherence to a Healthy Lifestyle, and Coronary Disease', *New England Journal of Medicine*, 15(24):2349–2358, doi.org/10.1056/NEJMoa1605086.

14 Booth FW, Roberts CK, and Laye MJ (2012) 'Lack of Exercise Is a Major Cause of Chronic Diseases', *Comprehensive Physiology*, 2(2):1143–211, doi.org/10.1002/cphy.c110025.

Chapter 6

1   Leong DP et al. (2015) 'Prognostic Value of Grip Strength: Findings from the Prospective Urban Rural Epidemiology (PURE) Study', *The Lancet*, 386(9990):266–273, https://www.thelancet.com/journals/lancet/article/PIIS0140-6736(14)62000-6.

2   O'Bryan SJ, Giuliano C, Woessner MN, Vogrin S, Smith C, Duque G, and Levinger I (2022) 'Progressive Resistance Training for Concomitant Increases in Muscle Strength and Bone Mineral Density in Older Adults: A Systematic Review and Meta-Analysis', *Sports Medicine*, 52(8):1939–1960, doi.org/10.1007/s40279-022-01675-2.

3   AFP (25 September 2015) 'Centenarian Hidekichi Miyazaki, Dubbed Golden Bolt, Sets Sprint Record in Japan', *ABC News*, accessed 24 September 2025, https://www.abc.net.au/news/2015-09-25/golden-bolt-hidekichi-miyazaki-sets-sprint-record/6804376.

4   Luu C and Wakatsuki Y (24 September 2015) 'Bet You Wish You Could Sprint at 105 – This Japanese Man Can', *CNN*, accessed 24 September 2025, https://edition.cnn.com/2015/09/24/asia/japan-cen-

tenarian-sprint-record.

5   Rowe P, Koller A, and Sharma S (2023) 'Physiology, Bone Remodeling', *StatPearls*, https://www.ncbi.nlm.nih.gov/books/NBK499863/.

6   Alnasser SM, Babakair RA, Al Mukhlid AF, Al Hassan SSS, Nuhmani S, and Muaidi Q (2025) 'Effectiveness of Exercise Loading on Bone Mineral Density and Quality of Life Among People Diagnosed with Osteoporosis, Osteopenia, and at Risk of Osteoporosis – A Systematic Review and Meta-Analysis', *Journal of Clinical Medicine*, 14(12):4109, https://doi.org/10.3390/jcm14124109.

7   Watson SL, Weeks BK, Weis LJ, Harding AT, Horan SA, and Beck BR (2018) 'High-Intensity Resistance and Impact Training Improves Bone Mineral Density and Physical Function in Postmenopausal Women with Osteopenia and Osteoporosis: The LIFTMOR Randomized Controlled Trial', *Journal of Bone and Mineral Research*, 33(2):211–220, https://doi.org/10.1002/jbmr.3284.

8   BMJ (2020) 'Effect of Exercise Training for Five Years on All Cause Mortality in Older Adults – the Generation 100 Study: Randomised Controlled Trial', *BMJ*, 371, doi.org/10.1136/bmj.m3485.

9   Jensen J, Rustad PI, Kolnes AJ, and Lai YC (2011) 'The Role of Skeletal Muscle Glycogen Breakdown for Regulation of Insulin Sensitivity by Exercise', *Frontiers in Physiology*, 30(2):112, doi.org/10.3389/fphys.2011.00112.

10   Ihalainen JK, Inglis A, Mäkinen T, Newton RU, Kainulainen H, Kyröläinen H, and Walker S (2019) 'Strength Training Improves Metabolic Health Markers in Older Individual Regardless of Training Frequency, Frontiers in Physiology, 10(32), doi.org/10.3389/fphys.2019.00032;
Lopez-Pedrosa JM, Camprubi-Robles M, Guzman-Rolo G, Lopez-Gonzalez A, Garcia-Almeida JM, Sanz-Paris A, and Rueda R (2024) 'The Vicious Cycle of Type 2 Diabetes Mellitus and Skeletal Muscle Atrophy: Clinical, Biochemical, and Nutritional Bases', *Nutrients*, 16(1):172, doi.org/10.3390/nu16010172.

11   Pedersen B and Febbraio M (2012) 'Muscles, Exercise and Obesity:

Skeletal Muscle as a Secretory Organ', *Nature Reviews Endocrinology*, 8:457–465, doi.org/10.1038/nrendo.2012.49.

12 Chen ML, Wu YJ, Lee MJ, Hsieh SL, Tseng IJ, Chen LS, and Gardenhire DS (2023) 'Effects of Resistance Exercise on Cognitive Performance and Depressive Symptoms in Community-Dwelling Older Chinese Americans: A Pilot Randomized Controlled Trial', *Behavioral Sciences*, 13(3):241, doi.org/10.3390/bs13030241.

13 Duckworth AL, Peterson C, Matthews MD and Kelly DR (2007) 'Grit: Perseverance and Passion for Long-Term Goals', *Journal of Personality and Social Psychology*, 92(6):1087–1101, doi.org/10.1037/0022-3514.92.6.1087.

Chapter 7

1   Hu P, Lee EKP, Li Q, Tam LS, Wong SYS, Poon PK, and Yip BHK (2025) 'Mediterranean Diet and Rheumatoid Arthritis: A Nine-Year Cohort Study and Systematic Review with Meta-Analysis', *European Journal of Clinical Nutrition*, 79:888–896, doi.org/10.1038/s41430-025-01628-8.

2   Longo V (2018) *The Longevity Diet: Discover the New Science Behind Stem Cell Activation and Regeneration to Slow Aging, Fight Disease, and Optimize Weight*, Avery Publishing Group.

3   Venetsanopoulou AI, Voulgari PV, and Drosos AA (2020) 'Fasting Mimicking Diets: A Literature Review of Their Impact on Inflammatory Arthritis', *Mediterranean Journal of Rheumatology*, 30(4):201–206, doi.org/10.31138/mjr.30.4.201.

4   Longo V (19 April 2025) 'Eventually, it will be possible to connect a person's DNA ...' [Facebook status], accessed 25 September 2025, https://www.facebook.com/profvalterlongo/posts/eventually-it-will-be-possible-to-connect-a-persons-dna-the-genome-to-the-food-h/1240215314134829/.

5   Willcox DC, Willcox BJ, Todoriki H, and Suzuki M (2009) 'The Okinawan Diet: Health Implications of a Low-Calorie, Nutrient-Dense, Antioxidant-Rich Dietary Pattern Low in Glycemic Load', *The Journal*

of the American College of Nutrition, 28:500S-516S, doi.org/10.1080/0 7315724.2009.10718117. PMID: 20234038.

6   Most J, Tosti V, Redman LM, and Fontana L (2017) 'Calorie Restriction in Humans: An Update', *Ageing Research Reviews*, 39:36–45, doi. org/10.1016/j.arr.2016.08.005.

7   ABC News (6 March 2015) 'World's Oldest Person Turns 117, Reveals Secret to Long Life', *ABC News,* accessed 26 September 2025, https://abcnews.go.com/Health/worlds-oldest-person-turns-117-reveals-secret-long/story?id=29409111.

8   Shirota M, Watanabe N, Suzuki M, and Kobori M (2008) 'Japanese-Style Diet and Cardiovascular Disease Mortality: A Systematic Review and Meta-Analysis of Prospective Cohort Studies', *Nutrients*, 14(10), doi.org/10.3390/nu14102008;
Tsugane S (2021) 'Why Has Japan Become the World's Most Long-Lived Country: Insights from a Food and Nutrition Perspective', *European Journal of Clinical Nutrition*, 75:921–928, doi.org/10.1038/ s41430-020-0677-5;
Otsuka R (2022) 'Diet, Nutrition, and Cognitive Function: A Narrative Review of Japanese Longitudinal Studies', *Geriatrics and Gerontology International*, 22(10):825–831, doi.org/10.1111/ggi.14463.

9   Dmitrieva NI, Boehm M, Yancey PH, and Enhörning S (2024) 'Long-Term Health Outcomes Associated with Hydration Status', *Nature Reviews Nephrology*, 20(5):275–294, doi.org/10.1038/s41581-024-00817-1.

10 Dmitrieva NI, Boehm M, Yancey PH, and Enhörning S (2024) 'Long-Term Health Outcomes Associated with Hydration Status', *Nature Reviews Nephrology*, 20(5):275–294, doi.org/10.1038/s41581-024-00817-1;
Allen MD, Springer DA, Burg MB, Boehm M, and Dmitrieva NI (2019) 'Suboptimal Hydration Remodels Metabolism, Promotes Degenerative Diseases, and Shortens Life', *JCI Insight,* 4(17), doi. org/10.1172/jci.insight.130949.

11 Harvard Health Publishing (n.d.) 'How Much Water Should You Drink?' *Harvard Medical School,* accessed 26 September 2025, https://

www.health.harvard.edu/staying-healthy/how-much-water-should-you-drink.

12 Poggiogalle E, Jamshed H, and Peterson CM (2018) 'Circadian Regulation of Glucose, Lipid, and Energy Metabolism in Humans', *Metabolism – Clinical and Experimental*, 84:11–27, https://www.metabolismjournal.com/article/S0026-0495(17)30329-3/abstract.

13 Jakubowicz D, Barnea M, Wainstein J, and Froy O (2013), 'High Caloric Intake at Breakfast vs. Dinner Differentially Influences Weight Loss of Overweight and Obese Women', *Obesity*, 21(12):2504–2512, doi.org/10.1002/oby.20460.

14 Wilkinson MJ et al. (2020) 'Ten-Hour Time-Restricted Eating Reduces Weight, Blood Pressure, and Atherogenic Lipids in Patients with Metabolic Syndrome', *Cell Metabolism*, 31(1):92–104, https://www.cell.com/cell-metabolism/fulltext/S1550-4131(19)30611-4.

15 Yamagata K (2019) 'Polyphenols Regulate Endothelial Functions and Reduce the Risk of Cardiovascular Disease', *Current Pharmaceutical Design*, 25(22):2443–2458, doi.org/10.2174/1381612825666190722100504;
Filosa S, Di Meo F, and Crispi S (2018) 'Polyphenols-Gut Microbiota Interplay and Brain Neuromodulation', *Neural Regeneration Research*, 13(12):2055–2059, doi.org/10.4103/1673-5374.241429.

16 Wei C, Zhang J, Chen N, Xu Z, and Tang H (2018) 'Does Frequent Tea Consumption Provide Any Benefit to Cognitive Function in Older Adults? Evidence From a National Survey from China in 2018', *Frontiers in Public Health*, 11, doi.org/10.3389/fpubh.2023.1269675.

17 WebMD Editorial Contributor (31 December 2024) 'Health Benefits of Chrysanthemum Tea', *WebMD*, accessed 26 September 2025, https://www.webmd.com/diet/health-benefits-chrysanthemum-tea.

Chapter 8

1 Cohen R, Chirag B, and Rozanski A (2016) 'Purpose in Life and Its Relationship to All-Cause Mortality and Cardiovascular Events:

A Meta-Analysis', *Psychosomatic Medicine,* 78(2):122–133, doi. org/10.1097/PSY.0000000000000274.

2   Shammas MA (2011) 'Telomeres, Lifestyle, Cancer, and Aging', *Current Opinion in Clinical Nutrition and Metabolic Care,* 14(1):28-34, doi.oeg/10.1097/MCO.0b013e32834121b1.

3   Resurgence (n.d.) 'The Story of Satish Kumar', accessed 26 September 2025, https://www.resurgence.org/education/media-resources/Resurgence-50-Satish-Kumars-Story.pdf.

4   Kumar S (2016) 'My Life on the Move', *Resurgence,* accessed 26 September 2025, https://www.resurgence.org/magazine/article4604-my-life-on-the-move.html.

5   Saint-Maurice PF, Troiano RP, Bassett DR Jr, Graubard BI, Carlson SA, Shiroma EJ, Fulton JE, and Matthews CE (2020) 'Association of Daily Step Count and Step Intensity with Mortality Among US Adults', *JAMA,* 323(12):1151–1160, doi.org/10.1001/jama.2020.1382.

6   Raichlen DA and Alexander GE (2017) 'Adaptive Capacity: An Evolutionary Neuroscience Model Linking Exercise, Cognition, and Brain Health', *Trends in Neuroscience*s, 40(7):408–421, doi.org/10.1016/j.tins.2017.05.001.

7   Morozink JA, Friedman EM, Coe CL, and Ryff CD (2010) 'Socioeconomic and Psychosocial Predictors of Interleukin-6 in the MIDUS National Sample', *Health Psychology,* 29(6):626–635, doi.org/10.1037/a0021360.

8   Rock 'n' Roll Running Series (19 November 2020) 'Remembering Harriette Thompson: 1923-2017', accessed 26 September 2025, https://www.runrocknroll.com/news/remembering-harriette-thompson-1923-2017.

9   Simpson D, Post PG, Young G, and Jensen PR (2014) '"It's Not About Taking the Easy Road": The Experiences of Ultramarathon Runners', *Sport Psychologist,* 28(2):176–185, doi.org/10.1123/tsp.2013-0064.

10 Teixeira PJ, Carraça EV, Markland D, Silva MN, and Ryan RM
    (2012) 'Exercise, Physical Activity, and Self-Determination Theory: A
    Systematic Review', *International Journal of Behavioural Nutrition and
    Physical Activity*, 9(78), doi.org/10.1186/1479-5868-9-78.

Chapter 9

1   Waldinger RJ and Schulz MS (2010) 'What's Love Got to Do with
    It? Social Functioning, Perceived Health, and Daily Happiness in
    Married Octogenarians', *Psychology and Aging*, 25(2):422–431, doi.
    org/10.1037/a0019087.

2   Frankl V (1946) *Man's Search for Meaning*, Beacon Press.

3   Reuters (14 March 2017) 'Record-Breaking Marathoner Ed Whitlock
    Dies at 86', *Reuters*, accessed 6 October 2025, https://www.reuters.
    com/article/sports/record-breaking-marathoner-ed-whitlock-dies-at-
    86-idUSKBN16K2QC/.

4   Douglas S (16 February 2010) 'Ed Whitlock and the Age of Simplic-
    ity', *Runner's World*, accessed 6 October 2025, https://www.runner-
    sworld.com/runners-stories/a20790188/ed-whitlock-and-the-age-of-
    simplicity/.

5   Robertson I and Cooper CL (2013) 'Resilience', *Stress and Health*,
    29(3):175–176, doi.org/10.1002/smi.2512. PMID: 23913839; Win-
    dle G (2011) 'What Is Resilience? A Review and Concept Analysis',
    Reviews in Clinical Gerontology, 21(2):152–169, doi.org/10.1017/
    S0959259810000420.

6   Hernández-Flórez N (2025) 'Running and Its Impact on Quali-
    ty of Life and Mental Health Through Mindfulness', *QVADRATA
    Estudios Sobre Educación Artes y Humanidades*, 7(14):93–105, doi.
    org/10.54167/qvadrata.v7i14.2052.

7   Newman V (29 August 2023) 'Japanese Skier Went on Incredible
    Journey to Become Oldest Man to Climb Everest', *Guiness World
    Records*, accessed 6 October 2025, https://www.guinnessworldrecords.
    com/news/2023/8/japanese-skier-went-on-incredible-journey-to-be-

come-oldest-man-to-climb-everest-757622.

8   Alexious G (29 August 2024) 'Paraplegic Ocean Rower Angela Madsen Celebrated in Upcoming Documentary', *Forbes,* accessed 6 October 2025, https://www.forbes.com/sites/gusalexiou/2024/08/29/paraplegic-ocean-rower-angela-madsen-celebrated-in-power-ful-new-documentary/.

9   Lesco J (30 August 2012) 'Ex-Marine Angela Madsen on Her Journey from Homelessness to the Paralympics', *NBC News,* accessed 6 October 2025, https://www.nbcnews.com/news/world/ex-marine-an-gela-madsen-her-journey-homelessness-paralympics-flna971591.

10 Alexious G (29 August 2024) 'Paraplegic Ocean Rower Angela Madsen Celebrated in Upcoming Documentary', *Forbes,* accessed 6 October 2025, https://www.forbes.com/sites/gusalexiou/2024/08/29/paraplegic-ocean-rower-angela-madsen-celebrated-in-power-ful-new-documentary/.

11 Alexious G (29 August 2024) 'Paraplegic Ocean Rower Angela Madsen Celebrated in Upcoming Documentary', *Forbes,* accessed 6 October 2025, https://www.forbes.com/sites/gusalexiou/2024/08/29/paraplegic-ocean-rower-angela-madsen-celebrated-in-power-ful-new-documentary/.

12 Kubota S (25 June 2020) 'Paralympian Angela Madsen Dies Try-ing to Row from LA to Hawaii', *Today,* accessed 7 October 2025, https://www.today.com/news/paralympian-angela-madsen-dies-try-ing-row-la-hawaii-t185125.

13 Tedeschi RG and Calhoun LG (2004) 'Posttraumatic Growth: Con-ceptual Foundations and Empirical Evidence', *Psychological Inquiry,* 15(1):1–18, doi.org/10.1207/s15327965pli1501_01.

14 Lee LO, James P, Zevon ES, et al. (2019) 'Optimism Is Associated with Exceptional Longevity in 2 Epidemiologic Cohorts of Men and Women', *PNAS,* 116(37):18357–18362, doi.org/10.1073/pnas.1900712116.

15 Epel ES et al. (2004) 'Accelerated Telomere Shortening in Response

to Life Stress', *PNAS*, 101(49): 17312–17315, doi.org/10.1073/pnas.0407162101.

16   McGonigal K (2016) *The Upside of Stress: Why Stress Is Good for You, and How to Get Good at It*, Avery.

17   Ryan RM and Deci EL (2000) 'Self-Determination Theory and the Facilitation of Intrinsic Motivation, Social Development, and Well-Being', *American Psychologist*, 55(1), 68–78, doi.org/10.1037/0003-066X.55.1.68.

18   Wang X, Jie W, Huang X, et al. (2024) 'Association of Psychological Resilience with All-Cause and Cause-Specific Mortality in Older Adults: A Cohort Study', *BMC Public Health*, 24(1):1989, doi.org/10.1186/s12889-024-19558-8.

19   Ye B, Li Y, Bao Z, and Gao J (2024) 'Psychological Resilience and Frailty Progression in Older Adults', *JAMA Network Open*, 7(11):e2447605, doi.org/10.1001/jamanetworkopen.2024.47605.

20   Martin J (2025) 'The Relationship Between Grit, Resilience and Physical Activity: A Systematic Review', *Frontiers in Sports and Active Living*, 7, doi.org/10.3389/fspor.2025.1563382.

21   Gazerani P (2025) 'The Neuroplastic Brain: Current Breakthroughs and Emerging Frontiers', *Brain Research*, 1858, doi.org/10.1016/j.brainres.2025.149643.

22   Fadare SA, Lambaco E, Mangrosi YB, and Louise LJD (2022) 'A Voyage into the Visualization of Athletic Performances: A Review', *American Journal of Multidisciplinary Research and Innovation*, 1(3):105–109, doi.org/10.54536/ajmri.v1i3.479.

23   Lally P, van Jaarsveld HM, Potts HWW, and Wardle J (2009) 'How Are Habits Formed: Modelling Habit Formation in the Real World', *European Journal of Social Psychology*, 40(6):998–1009, doi.org/10.1002/ejsp.674.

24   Troy AS, Wilhelm FH, Shallcross AJ, and Mauss IB (2010) 'Seeing the Silver Lining: Cognitive Reappraisal Ability Moderates the Relationship Between Stress and Depressive Symptoms', *Emotion*,

10(6):783–795, doi.org/10.1037/a0020262.

25 Meichenbaum D (2007) 'Stress Inoculation Training: A Preventative and Treatment Approach.', in Lehrer PM, Woolfolk RL, and Sime WE (eds), *Principles and Practice of Stress Management*, 3rd edn, The Guilford Press.

26 Holt-Lunstad J (2024) 'Social Connection as a Critical Factor for Mental and Physical Health: Evidence, Trends, Challenges, and Future Implications', *World Psychiatry*, 23(3):312–332, doi.org/10.1002/wps.21224.

27 Seery MD (2011) 'Resilience: A Silver Lining to Experiencing Adverse Life Events?', *Current Directions in Psychological Science*, 20(6):390–394, doi.org/10.1177/0963721411424740.

Chapter 10

1 Uchino BN (2006) 'Social Support and Health: A Review of Physiological Processes Potentially Underlying Links to Disease Outcomes', *Journal of Behavioral Medicine*, 29(4):377–87, doi.org/10.1007/s10865-006-9056-5.

2 Holt-Lunstad J, Smith TB, Baker M, Harris T, and Stephenson D (2015) 'Loneliness and Social Isolation as Risk Factors for Mortality: A Meta-Analytic Review', *Perspectives on Psychological Science*, 10(2):227–37, doi.org/10.1177/1745691614568352; Novotney A (May 2019) 'The Risks of Social Isolation', *APA,* accessed 7 October 2025, https://www.apa.org/monitor/2019/05/ce-corner-isolation.

3 Kotifani A (2018) 'Moai – This Tradition Is Why Okinawan People Live Better, Longer', *Blue Zones,* accessed 7 October 2025, https://www.bluezones.com/2018/08/moai-this-tradition-is-why-okinawan-people-live-longer-better/.

4 Holt-Lunstad J, Smith TB, and Layton JB (2010) 'Social Relationships and Mortality Risk: A Meta-Analytic Review', *PLoS Medicine*, 7(7):e1000316, doi.org/10.1371/journal.pmed.1000316.

5 Waldinger RJ and Schulz MS (2010) 'What's Love Got to Do with

It? Social Functioning, Perceived Health, and Daily Happiness in Married Octogenarians', *Psychology and Aging,* 25(2):422–431, doi. org/10.1037/a0019087.

6   Express (18 September 2017) 'Secret to Long Life? 111-Year-Old Says Drinking THIS Has Kept Her Feeling Young', *Express,* accessed 8 October 2025, https://www.express.co.uk/news/uk/855662/Britain-oldest-people-Grace-Jones-whiskey.

7   Ong AD, Mann FD, and Kubzansky LD (2025) 'Cumulative Social Advantage Is Associated with Slower Epigenetic Aging and Lower Systemic Inflammation', *Brain, Behavior, & Immunity,* 48, doi. org/10.1016/j.bbih.2025.101096.

8   Fratiglioni L, Paillard-Borg S, and Winblad B (2004) 'An Active and Socially Integrated Lifestyle in Late Life Might Protect Against Dementia', *The Lancet Neurology,* 3(6):343–353, https://www.thelancet. com/journals/laneur/article/PIIS1474-4422(04)00767-7/.

9   Holt-Lunstad J, Smith TB, and Layton JB (2010) 'Social Relationships and Mortality Risk: A Meta-Analytic Review', *PLoS Medicine,* 7(7):e1000316, doi.org/10.1371/journal.pmed.1000316.

10   Waldinger RJ and Schulz MS (2010) 'What's Love Got to Do with It? Social Functioning, Perceived Health, and Daily Happiness in Married Octogenarians', *Psychology and Aging,* 25(2):422–431, doi. org/10.1037/a0019087.

11   Kuiper JS, Zuidersma M, Oude Voshaar RC, Zuidema SU, van den Heuvel ER, Stolk RP, and Smidt N (2015) 'Social Relationships and Risk of Dementia: A Systematic Review and Meta-Analysis of Longitudinal Cohort Studies', *Ageing Research Reviews,* 22:39–57, doi.org/ 10.1016/j.arr.2015.04.006.

12   Waldinger RJ and Schulz MS (2010) 'What's Love Got to Do with It? Social Functioning, Perceived Health, and Daily Happiness in Married Octogenarians', *Psychology and Aging,* 25(2):422–431, doi. org/10.1037/a0019087.

13 Naito R (2023) 'Social Isolation as a Risk Factor for All-Cause Mortality: Systematic Review and Meta-Analysis of Cohort Studies', *PLOS One,* doi.org/10.1371/journal.pone.0280308.

14 Glover L, Sutton J, O'Brien E, and Sims M (2023) 'Social Networks and Cardiovascular Disease Events in the Jackson Heart Study', *Journal of the American Heart Association,* 12(22):e030149, doi:10.1161/JAHA.123.030149.

15 Mahalingam G, Samtani S, Lam BCP et al. (2023) 'Social Connections and Risk of Incident Mild Cognitive Impairment, Dementia, and Mortality in 13 Longitudinal Cohort Studies of Ageing', *Alzheimer's and Dementia Journal,* 19:5114–5128, doi.org/10.1002/alz.13072.

16 Heinrichs M, Baumgartner T, Kirschbaum C, and Ehlert U (2003) 'Social Support and Oxytocin Interact to Suppress Cortisol and Subjective Responses to Psychosocial Stress', *Biological Psychiatry,* 54(12):1389–98, doi.org/10.1016/s0006-3223(03)00465-7.

Chapter 11

1 Okun MA, Yeung EW, and Brown S (2013) 'Volunteering by Older Adults and Risk of Mortality: A Meta-Analysis', *Psychology and Aging,* 28(2):564–77, doi.org/10.1037/a0031519.

2 Christakis NA and Fowler JH (2007) 'The Spread of Obesity in a Large Social Network Over 32 Years', *New England Journal Medicine,* 357(4):370–9, doi.org/10.1056/NEJMsa066082.

3 Du T and Li Y (2022) 'Effects of Social Networks in Promoting Young Adults' Physical Activity among Different Sociodemographic Groups', *Behavioral Science,* 12(9):345, doi.org/10.3390/bs12090345.

www.ingramcontent.com/pod-product-compliance
Lightning Source LLC
Chambersburg PA
CBHW031846200326
41597CB00012B/290